SECRETS TO BUILDING
PEOPLE AND TEAMS THAT
WIN CONSISTENTLY

✦ ✦ ✦

THE
MENTOR
LEADER

TONY DUNGY

WITH

NATHAN WHITAKER

TYNDALE HOUSE PUBLISHERS, INC.
CAROL STREAM, ILLINOIS

Visit Tyndale's exciting Web site at www.tyndale.com.

TYNDALE and Tyndale's quill logo are registered trademarks of Tyndale House Publishers, Inc.

The Mentor Leader: Secrets to Building People and Teams That Win Consistently

Designed by Dean H. Renninger

Edited by Dave Lindstedt

Published in association with the literary agency of Legacy, LLC, Winter Park, Florida 32789.

Library of Congress Cataloging-in-Publication Data

Dungy, Tony.
    The mentor leader : secrets to building people and teams that win consistently / Tony Dungy with Nathan Whitaker.
        p. cm.
    ISBN 978-1-4143-3804-0 (hc)
    1. Leadership—Religious aspects—Christianity. 2. Mentoring—Religious aspects—Christianity.
3. Leadership. 4. Mentoring. I. Whitaker, Nathan. II. Title.
    BV4597.53.L43D86 2010
    158'.4—dc22   2010020832

Printed in the United States of America

16   15   14   13   12   11   10
 7   6   5   4   3   2   1

CONTENTS

FOREWORD

by Jim Caldwell

On Friday, November 17, 2006, two days before a big game against the Dallas Cowboys, head coach Tony Dungy received word through our security officers that a party was going to take place and that many of our players would be in attendance. As you can imagine, once this party was publicized, it would draw a crowd of great Colts fans who wanted to be in the midst of the action, but also others who may have had different motives.

The Indianapolis Colts have not had many players who have run afoul of the law—and there are distinct reasons why. Number one, under the leadership of owner Jim Irsay, president Bill Polian, and Tony, the team had a policy of placing character in the forefront of the player-selection process. It was a common organizational practice to eliminate players—even talented "difference-makers"—from consideration in the draft if they possessed questionable character flaws. Number two, the team is committed to purposeful, effective communication. Tony began most team meetings by reminding everyone to refrain from questionable behavior. To emphasize his point, he used an overhead projector to display newspaper clippings involving other professional athletes who had been arrested or accused of illegal activity. He highlighted the circumstances surrounding the incidents and discussed ways to avoid a similar fate.

During our customary 9 a.m. team meeting that Friday, Tony warned the team about the party scheduled for that evening. He drove the point home clearly and succinctly: "We do not need any distractions." We were undefeated, 9–0 to be exact, and we were traveling to Dallas the next day. As the saying goes, forewarned is forearmed, but not all our guys got the message.

At the party, an altercation occurred and one of our team members put himself in a position to be detained by the police. Though some of the details are still rather sketchy and remain unanswered, it involved a contentious exchange with a woman at the party.

As you can imagine, the incident did not sit well with Tony. The violation appeared to fly in the face of his warning, and he was not amused. Tony rarely displays a visible reaction to uncomfortable situations, but if you had been around him as long as I have, you would have sensed his displeasure.

On Saturday morning, before our flight to Dallas, Tony met with the young man, and he later made the team aware of the incident. He said he didn't know exactly how he was going to respond, but there would be consequences. He later handled the situation privately with the individual involved.

After the 2005 season, I had a few NFL teams contact me about their head coaching positions. Those inquiries didn't result in a job offer, but in order to prepare myself for future opportunities and the possibility of one day leading an NFL franchise, I asked Tony if he would mind if I came into his office periodically to ask him a question or two about the role of head coach. He was always so gracious, and he agreed enthusiastically to my request.

The Thursday after the Dallas game, when I went in to ask Tony a few questions about managing the team, I also asked him whether he was inclined to demonstrate a show of force in response to the incident from the previous week. His simple five-word reply—"It is not about me"—resonated with my spirit, and it is one of the most profound lessons I learned from him.

A typical leader might have tried to maintain his posture of authority in front of the team by "saber-rattling" and creating a scene as a deterrent—pounding on the podium and making an example of the player, in response to the infraction. But Tony took an alternate approach. As long as the player got the message and learned from his mistake, Tony was more interested in what was most important for the team and the franchise.

By the way, he never had another issue with that young man. The two of them share a unique bond today, and they continue to stay in touch.

In his book *Good to Great*, Jim Collins identifies the characteristics of highly effective companies and companies that fail. While conducting his research, he found that chief executive officers of the effective companies had similar traits—which Collins calls Level 5 leadership traits. The description of the Level 5 leader sums up Tony's leadership DNA perfectly:

> Level 5 leaders . . .
>> embody a paradoxical mix of personal humility and professional will.
>> display a compelling modesty, are self-effacing and understated.
>> attribute success to factors other than themselves.
>> display a workmanlike diligence—more plow horse than show horse.
>> attribute success to factors other than themselves.
>> set up their successors for even greater success.*

I will say "amen" to that. Tony graciously empowered me and others

---

*Jim Collins, *Good to Great* (New York: HarperBusiness, 2001), 39.

to reach our full potential and take ownership of the team's success. He was an active participant in our development, and he checked his ego at the door. He was more likely to ask questions than make decrees.

Subsequent to Tony's retirement, I have often been asked, "How will you fill those big shoes?" My response has been, "I don't have to do it alone." There is only one Tony Dungy, Joe Paterno, or Chuck Noll. The leadership style that Tony employed allowed for a sense of autonomy, development, growth, understanding, and ownership.

Furthermore, with the Colts, we have an excellent owner who knows the business inside and out. We have an elite personnel department that is experienced and knowledgeable and always two steps ahead of the curve. We have a great coaching staff of outstanding teachers. We have a group of players who listen to every word we say, and they believe in our formula for winning. We have veteran leadership that has taken ownership of the team, setting a businesslike tone with unparalleled work habits.

Because of Tony's leadership style, he allowed those around him to function in an atmosphere where autonomy was the rule and not the exception. He nurtured and cultivated both players and coaches, molding without pressing, nudging without pushing, and leading without dragging.

Having worked with Tony and learned from him made my job a lot easier in the first year after his retirement. All I had to do was tweak a few things to match my own personality and then manage from the middle, as I had seen Tony do, and not be fearful of empowering those around me. Observing Tony during the eight years we worked together was truly a blessing. Now you have an opportunity to see why success was so prevalent under his reign, and to witness the impact his leadership style had on everyone around him. I daresay that, after you've read this book, you will be impacted profoundly as well.

ACKNOWLEDGMENTS

Once again, Tony and I recognize that we could not have done it alone. And once again, Tony is reluctant to single out individuals because of his concern—borne out by the feedback we've received from our prior books' acknowledgments—that we will overlook someone. However, I will try once again, fueled by the knowledge that, though Tony could have pulled this off by himself, once I was involved—as those who know me well will recognize—there must have been a village behind our efforts to save it and make it a decent read.

Our gratitude extends beyond the names listed below, to those who have supported our endeavor in so many ways. Those who went beyond the call of duty include:

Donald Miller, who graciously gave of his time to share his passion for mentoring.

John Streitmatter, of Leadership Research Institute, and Heath Schiesser for generously reviewing the manuscript to keep us from misrepresenting the latest in leadership research. If we have persisted in making errors, it is despite their best efforts.

D. J. Snell, our literary agent and partner in our literary undertakings, from the inception of the idea to the completion of the work and beyond.

Our steadfast partners at Tyndale House, including but not limited to Doug Knox and Jan Long Harris, who convinced Tony that this was a topic he needed to tackle; Dave Lindstedt, Sarah Atkinson, Bonne Steffen, Jonathan Schindler, Yolanda Sidney, Nancy Clausen, and Todd Starowitz.

Jessica Quinn, who has been such a loyal partner in each of our projects.

Scott Whitaker, whose leadership insights helped me develop initial concepts, and whose wordsmithery—both in the drafting and editing stages—helped bring this book into being.

And, once again, to our wives, Lauren and Amy, and our children, Tiara, Eric, Hannah, Jordan, Jade, Ellie Kate, Justin, and Jason, for your patience and for filling our homes with such joyful, delightful distractions as we worked.

INTRODUCTION

If all you're about is winning, it's not really worth it.
I'm after things that last.
KELI MCGREGOR

It was still raining steadily, but my thoughts were far away from the weather. While still captured by the euphoria of the moment, I turned philosophical, thinking, "How did I get here?" Of all the people who could have been headed up the steps to the podium to accept the Lombardi trophy for winning Super Bowl XLI, it was *me*. As soon as I thought it, though, I knew it wasn't only me. Instead, it was a combination of my mom and dad, Lauren, Allen Truman, Dave Driscoll, Leroy Rockquemore, Cal Stoll, Donnie Shell, John Stallworth, Chuck Noll, Richard Farmer, Denny Green, Rich McKay, Bill Polian, and so many others who had, for whatever reason, built into my life.

I had been mentored by so many. They had all added value to my life. And my leadership style had been influenced by them. I had thought about the idea of leading in such a way that it created value for others, but in that moment, thinking of so many people who had made a difference in my life and had so much to do with my being on that podium in that steady drizzle, the idea of mentoring crystallized for me. It isn't a structured program that necessarily makes the difference; rather, the difference is made moment by moment by leaders who care—for others.

As I hoisted that trophy above my head, I realized the responsibility we all have to become mentor leaders in the lives of others.

Most people, at one time or another in their lives, will take on the role of a leader—whether formally or informally, at work, at home, or at church. And most people, if they're honest about it, would say they feel a little inadequate in that role—whether as a parent or a boss or a team leader. Actually, some self-doubt is a healthy attribute in a leader.

Leadership is necessary in any human society; thus, a leadership void will not exist for very long before someone steps up to lead, either by popular acclaim, selection, or self-appointment. The question is, what type of leader will that person be?

This question is more than academic, however, for the leadership style can dictate how effective that person will be, and how significant an impact the person's leadership will create.

In my life and career, I have seen all kinds of leaders, but the ones who have had the greatest positive impact on my life are the select few who have been not only leaders but also mentors. In fact, it is largely because of the influence of mentors in my life that I was drawn to write this book.

I believe that certain principles of successful leadership are timeless. In other words, they're not just the latest fad or fashion, and they're not dependent on or dictated by our circumstances. Furthermore,

I have come to realize that these principles can be taught, learned, absorbed, and then passed on to others, especially to those whom we ourselves have the privilege to lead.

Conventional wisdom says that leaders are born, but I don't believe that's true. From what I've seen, positive, life-changing leadership is an acquired trait, learned from interaction with others who know how to lead and lead well. Leadership is not an innate, mystical gift; rather, it is a learned ability to influence the attitudes and behavior of others. As such, we can all learn—and then teach others—how to understand and apply the principles of successful leadership.

I spoke with the head of a Fortune 300 company who noted that he had recently experienced an awakening in how he interacted with his employees. He said, "I had long known that I could influence whether or not my employees had a good day; it was fairly obvious that I held sway over that, for better or worse. But one day, as I drove home, trying to fight off a dark cloud from a tough day's work and trying not to let it affect my family when I walked through the front door, I realized that many, if not all, of my direct reports were experiencing the same thing. If they weren't able to compartmentalize their frustration, anger, and irritation, then they were going to take those toxic feelings into their homes. I don't simply have an impact on my direct reports—there is an exponential effect on those around them as well, based in no small part on their interactions with me."

Understanding the profound effect of our leadership is often the first step toward adopting a style of leadership that has proved itself effective over many generations—a style I'm calling *mentor leadership*. It isn't so much the creation of a new kind of leadership as it is a recognition and exploration of a model I've learned—and tried to practice—throughout my life.

Much of what I've learned I owe to two men in particular: my father, Wilbur Dungy, who provided a consistent model for me through his teaching, coaching, and parenting; and Chuck Noll, my head coach when I was a player and an assistant coach with the Pittsburgh Steelers.

They, in turn, were shaped by others—my father by my grandfather, Herbert Dungy, who modeled for my dad what he in turn modeled for my siblings and me; and Coach Noll by Paul Brown and Don Shula, coaches under whom he coached and played.

As their title suggests, mentor leaders seek to have a direct, intentional, and positive impact on those they lead. At its core, mentoring is about building character into the lives of others, modeling and teaching attitudes and behaviors, and creating a constructive legacy to be passed along to future generations of leaders. I don't think it's possible to be an accidental mentor.

While leading in such an intentional manner, mentor leaders cannot help but also have a positive impact on others—whether as role models or through the lives of the people they have mentored. The primary focus of mentor leadership, however, is to shape the lives of the people right in front of them, as they lead, guide, inspire, and encourage those people.

We often mirror what we see. Coaches will model the behavior of successful coaches they know or observe, sometimes with detrimental results. Similarly, business leaders model other business leaders—or when necessary, try to do the opposite, whatever that might be.

Too often, though, we choose people to mirror or model, and leadership books to read, solely for the purpose of figuring out how to win more games or increase our financial bottom line. In the process of looking for leadership models to emulate, we choose people who have won a lot of games or who have made a lot of money for themselves or their organizations, with little thought given to how they have affected the lives of the people around them. If along the way lives are made better, we too often view it as a wonderful by-product rather than as a primary purpose of leadership.

I don't have all the answers, but my hope is that you'll find enough here that will help you become a positive mentor leader in whatever setting you find yourself.

Before we get into the heart of our discussion, here are some essential traits of a mentor leader to keep in mind:

- Becoming a mentor leader is not rocket science. If it were, *I* wouldn't be writing a book about leadership. As we'll see, leadership consists of principles and skills that are accessible to anyone and everyone. They aren't necessarily intuitive, but they aren't terribly difficult, either.
- Mentor leadership can be taught and learned; but in order to be absorbed, it must be practiced. The best way to evaluate leadership philosophies and find your own style is by testing them in action. You can't stay in the ivory tower reading books and discussing theories. Eventually you have to wade into the fray.
- Mentor leadership focuses on developing the strengths of individuals. It might be in a fairly narrow way, such as building a specific skill, or more broadly focused, such as teaching employees to be proactive about meeting others' needs so they can better support the organization. Successful mentor leaders make the people they lead better players, workers, students, or family members—and ultimately, better people.
- Mentor leadership works best when the ones being mentored are aware that the mentor leader has a genuine concern for their development and success. Those we lead will be more receptive if they believe we genuinely want them to succeed.

Though true mentor leadership is intentional, we need to understand that people are watching us and learning from us whether we're aware of it or not. The leadership we model can lead to positive or negative results. We've all seen cases where leaders have unintentionally fostered destructive, dysfunctional, or damaging behaviors. Parents who have heard their children echo harsh words to a pet, doll, or sibling will know what I mean.

Success for a mentor leader is measured by different standards than those commonly accepted in our society. Mentor leadership is all about shaping, nurturing, empowering, and growing. It's all about relationships, integrity, and perpetual learning. Success is measured in changed lives, strong character, and eternal values rather than in material gain, temporal achievement, or status. Ultimately, mentor leadership is just as successful in achieving the standards of accomplishment in our society. But unlike other types of leadership, it is primarily concerned with building and adding value to the lives of people in the process.

It's about changing lives.

A Mentor Leader.

CHAPTER 1

THE MANDATE OF A MENTOR LEADER: FOCUS ON SIGNIFICANCE

You've got to do your own growing, no matter how tall your grandfather was.

OLD IRISH PROVERB

On January 24, 2010, as I sat in the stands at Lucas Oil Stadium, watching the Indianapolis Colts celebrate their victory over the New York Jets in the AFC Championship Game, I couldn't help but reflect on my relationships with the five men who now stood on the podium at midfield, handing the championship trophy from one man to the next—owner Jim Irsay, general manager Bill Polian, head coach Jim Caldwell, and team captains Peyton Manning and Gary Brackett.

I felt a measure of satisfaction that day, knowing that each of these leaders—along with the rest of the team—had committed to a common vision and a common goal at the beginning of the season. The goal, of course, was to win a championship, but along with that, everyone was concerned with raising the performance of all the others, with helping them become better players, better coaches, and better men. Each man had a different role and responsibility in accomplishing that goal, but they had all been united in purpose and in their pursuit of excellence. And now they were able to celebrate their success together.

Not only were these men leaders in a positional sense within the organization—and thus were enjoying the team's success—but they had also embraced the principles of mentor leadership and were leaders in a relational sense as well. If they hadn't established the types of relationships they had with each other and with the other coaches and team members, but had only counted wins and losses, they would not have had the same level of positive influence on each other, and the season would not have been as successful. But I knew these men were good, grounded people, whose desire in everything they did was to make each other better—which, in my view, is a more accurate measure of success than wins and losses. It is also a defining characteristic of a mentor leader.

Unity of purpose and a desire to make other people better must start at the top if these goals are going to ripple through an entire organization. But, unfortunately, the opposite is equally true. I think we've all seen examples of the head coach who sits down at the table in the media room after the game, still basking in the afterglow of the big win. Behind him is the backdrop with the team logo and the corporate sponsor of the day, and as the coach answers the reporters' questions, he uses words such as *we*, *us*, and *our*, but what he really means is *I*, *me*, and *my*. And everyone on his team knows it—from the assistant coaches, who are often pushed aside or belittled in practice; to the players, who incur the coach's wrath if they do not perform

> ✦ Unity of purpose and a desire to make other people better must start at the top if these goals are going to ripple through an entire organization.

exactly as expected; to the members of the support staff, who are treated as less than human; to the families, who are not allowed anywhere near the workplace for fear they'll cause a loss of focus—or worse, that their presence might reorient the team's priorities away from winning games. After a while, people see through the talk when it doesn't line up with the walk.

When a team wins or a business is successful, the families of the players or the workers may be excited for the moment; but when they count the cost, I wonder how many would say that the temporary accomplishment outweighs all the memories missed or the bonds not formed. Or, worse yet, maybe they have been programmed over time to believe that the all-encompassing sacrifice of family, community, time—or anything other than what it takes to win games, close sales, or build a business—is an accepted part of life, simply what is required to achieve the number one priority: *winning*.

Sadly, such "accomplishment" without significance will ultimately prove to be meaningless and without lasting value. Mentor leaders insist on more and define success in a much more robust and well-rounded way.

MENTOR LEADERS PUT PEOPLE FIRST

Don't copy the behavior and customs of this world, but let God transform you into a new person by changing the way you think. Then you will learn to know God's will for you, which is good and pleasing and perfect.
ROMANS 12:2

Shortsighted leadership focuses primarily on the bottom line. In football, it's wins and losses and playoff berths. In business, it's quarterly profits, shareholder equity, and sales targets. Not that these things aren't important—they are. But when they become the primary focus of a business or a team, they inevitably result in an organization that is out of balance. Leaders whose definition of success depends on such a short-term focus—and by *short-term* I mean temporal, noneternal—will one day wake up to discover they've missed out on what is truly important in life, namely, meaningful relationships.

When life in the workplace is all about results and outcomes, it's easy to adopt the same mind-set in other venues as well. Thus, we have parents who scream at the umpire at Little League games, or browbeat their kids into getting straight A's, or harp on the players they coach in Pee Wee football about being "mentally tough." At home, in the limited time left for family, they're tempted to criticize if the house isn't just so or to cram in everything they want their spouses or kids to know, instead of taking time to build the kind of family relationships that God intends.

✛ **Shortsighted leadership focuses primarily on the bottom line.**

In our society, whether we'll admit it or not, the prevailing attitude is that the ends justify the means. We tell ourselves that "quality time" can make up for a lack of quantity time and that as long as we achieve whatever temporary, worldly goal we're pursuing, all is well. Just keep climbing. We think our spouses and kids need us first to be successful, and then we'll have time to be an important part of their lives.

We rationalize this kind of fuzzy thinking until we really begin to believe that our example, our impact, and our value to others—family, friends, and coworkers—are measured by what we produce and by the worldly things we accumulate. Our society loves and respects awards, degrees, money, status, achievement, and image. Just look at the accolades we heap upon business tycoons, movie stars, professional athletes . . . and football coaches.

But without meaningful relationships, relationships we invest ourselves in, what does it all amount to?

That's an easy one to answer: *dust.*

If you take only one thing from this book, let it be this: Relationships are ultimately what matter—our relationships with God and with other people. The key to becoming a mentor leader is learning how to put other people first. You see, the question that burns in the heart of the mentor leader is simply this: *What can I do to make other people better, to make them all that God created them to be?*

A life spent focused on things of the world will not add value to the lives of others.

Instead of asking, how can I lead my company, my team, or my family to a higher level of success? we should be asking ourselves, how do others around me flourish as a result of my leadership? Do they flourish at all? How does my leadership, my involvement in their lives—in whatever setting we're in—have a positive and lasting influence and impact on them?

If influence, involvement, improvement, and impact are core principles of mentor leadership, how can we make them central to everything we do? That's the question I intend to answer in the pages to follow.

Simply stated, leadership is influence. By influencing another person, we lead that person. Leadership is not dependent on a formal position or role. We can find opportunities for leadership wherever we go. Likewise, leadership is not based on manipulation or prescription, though sometimes it may appear that way to an outside observer. By keeping our motives aligned with doing the best for those around us, we will keep ourselves focused on being a positive influence.

✛ **Relationships are ultimately what matter– our relationships with God and with other people.**

I recognize that the world is not necessarily lacking in leadership books. There is certainly no shortage in the bookstores—and everyone from professors with PhDs to "successful" business executives to politicians and entrepreneurs have gotten in on the act.

Even football coaches have joined the crowd of voices espousing leadership principles—or at least ideas for winning football games. Many of these authors have good things to share, but most are not *other-oriented* enough for me. Maybe I've missed something, but most leadership books I've seen are too much about the leader, too much about the "me." Too much about improving the bottom line or upgrading the readers' status as leaders instead of having a positive impact on those they are called to lead. I once heard an executive say in an interview, "Of course I know how to lead. I've been in charge of one thing or another for the last thirty years." It may well be that this person knows how to lead, but simply "being in charge" is not evidence of leadership or leadership ability.

So much of what has been written about leadership focuses on *positional* leadership, that is, that one's status, or being in charge, determines whether one is a leader. But you don't have to look very far to see examples of people at the top of organizational charts who have very few leadership skills. Think about it: It's much easier to look like a leader when your followers know they can be fired for noncompliance or disobedience. But that type of oversight, governance, direction, and supervision is not what I mean when I talk about leadership—and, in particular, mentor leadership. Mentor leaders understand that if we lose sight of people, we lose sight of the very purpose of leadership.

One's position, or status, can supply part of the equation, but that is only a piece. In fact, many of the most effective leaders I've seen do not have positional authority over the people they lead. In my experience, some of the best examples of mentor leadership come from men and women whose influence extends to people who are not their subordinates.

> ✛ If we lose sight of people, we lose sight of the very purpose of leadership.

Mentor leadership focuses on relationships and positive influence because success in temporal things can be so fleeting. At the end of it all, sometimes you reach the organizational goals you've set, and sometimes you don't. But either way, if you're a leader, people's lives should be better because of the influence you've had along the way.

MENTOR LEADERS STRIVE FOR SIGNIFICANCE IN LIFE

Young kids with positive male role models have something to live for, somebody who is proud of them, somebody who cares about their well-being.

DONALD MILLER

If you follow professional football, or just read the news, you're probably familiar with the story of Michael Vick. A star quarterback with elusive speed and remarkable athleticism, Michael was drafted by the Atlanta Falcons in 2001 and quickly built a reputation as a game-breaker in the NFL. Then, in April 2007, word surfaced that a dog-fighting operation had been uncovered at a house Michael owned in his home state of Virginia. Though Michael initially denied any involvement with the dogfighting enterprise, he later pleaded guilty to federal charges and served twenty-one months in prison. After his release, I had an opportunity to meet with Michael and mentor him, and we established a relationship that continues to this day.

Because of the controversial nature of Michael's crime and his later reinstatement to the National Football League, I have been asked more times than I can remember why I got involved with him. I have answered those questions as candidly as I could, time and again, but I want to expand on my answer here because it is so critical to my approach to this discussion of mentor leadership.

To all appearances, Michael Vick was wildly successful—wealthy, at the top of his profession, and in the public eye. But as we all learned, there was more to the story. For all his worldly success, was he building a life of significance?

Leadership, as I believe it should be understood and displayed, must first and foremost recognize that it is not enough to be successful in the world's eyes. I've heard sociologist Tony Campolo say that the world has "switched the price tags," giving value to the valueless while undervaluing the truly important. Accumulating things is highly prized in our society, as are status and fame. On the other hand, the truly important things of life often happen in quiet, private moments—moments of faith, family, and building relationships.

Before his time in prison, I'm sure there were times when Michael thought about what a great opportunity God had given him. I know he thought about his family, his teammates, and the fans all over the country who looked up to him. But I don't think he ever contemplated the responsibility that goes along with a leadership position, whether in leading his family or his team, or in being a role model for so many other young men.

✢ **Leadership must first and foremost recognize that it is not enough to be successful in the world's eyes.**

When Michael's successful career was brought to a halt and he had time to think about it, he came to the conclusion that he hadn't done his part as a leader. God had blessed him with uncommon talent, and Michael had used it to rise to the top of his profession. Unfortunately, he realized he hadn't helped the people around him as much as he could have. And he wanted to do that—starting with his family, and then, he hoped, with another football team, if he were given the opportunity. But he also wanted to reach out to all the young boys who looked up to him, who wore his jersey, and who wrote him letters while he was in prison asking why he wasn't playing anymore. Could he still do those things? Could he still have that impact for good?

That's why I chose to work with Michael Vick. That's why I got involved in his life. I saw a young man in need, and I had an opportunity to do something. But more than that, I accepted the responsibility to perhaps provide a moment of significance in his life—a moment that would help him get his life back on track. I did what so many others had done for me—the things that have helped me become more the person I am and the person I want to be than I ever could have done on my own. You never know how these things will turn out, but you've got to be willing to try. My goal was to build into Michael Vick's life what I believe is important, things that Michael himself says he wants in his life—being close to his family, modeling good values for kids, and even speaking out against the animal cruelty that he now knows is wrong. Whether Michael ever regains the status and standing he once had in the NFL is not as important as what kind of man he becomes. Mentor leadership focuses on building people up, building significance into their lives, and building leaders for the next generation.

As you build your leadership skills, it's important to remember that *why* you lead is as important as *whom* you lead. Leading for the benefit of others is a much more compelling and powerful motivation than leading merely to get ahead or to hit an arbitrary target. Leadership based on building significance into the lives of others is much more energizing in the long term than other types of leadership. The very nature of mentor leadership is that it endures and can be replicated. As we build into the lives of the people around us, one at a time, one-on-one, we have the potential to extend our positive influence *through them* into countless other people as well.

✛ **Mentor leadership focuses on building people up and building leaders for the next generation.**

Mentor leadership isn't focused on self or solely on short-term goals like wins, championships, stock prices, or possessions; it is focused instead on the longer-term goal of bettering people's lives. And that includes people who have made mistakes, who have made a mess of their lives. Mentor leaders see potential and strive to develop it in the people they lead.

Michael Vick and I have pressed on with the goal of putting his life on a different and more significant trajectory. My primary goal is to build into his life so that he, in turn, can have a positive impact on other young men. Nothing would please me more than to see him become a mentor to other people in his own sphere of influence.

Because of my experience in the NFL and the fact that Michael Vick and I knew many people in common, I had the opportunity to work with him. But most mentoring relationships will not take place in the public spotlight. In fact, in order for mentoring to be genuine and effective, it should be a part of your everyday leadership style. In whatever setting you find yourself, you should strive to build into the lives of the people around you. The goal is to begin building leaders to take your place someday—to build leaders who will be equipped not only to lead your organization or some aspect of it, but also, when they leave your organization one day, to stand on their own and lead and build other people and organizations.

The personal, one-on-one aspect of mentoring is something our society desperately needs. I'm heavily involved in prison ministry, and far too often I see the results of a lack of mentoring. It is clearly a pattern in the early lives of the men and women who end up incarcerated. As I listen to their stories, it becomes clear that a mentor could have made a difference—just someone who cared enough to guide them, to be a positive influence, at their most vulnerable time. Instead, they sit day after day in a jail cell, hoping to someday get a second chance. Seeing lives and potential wasted is what makes me so passionate about developing mentor leaders.

There are those who don't want to admit it, but one of the most undervalued areas in our society today is the family unit. A number of studies have underscored the importance of a stable family in producing stable adults and a stable society. Statistics show that many of those incarcerated in our nation's jails and prisons grew up without fathers. Abe Brown, who founded the prison ministry in Florida that I've had the privilege to assist with, estimates that 70 percent of the men in prison today grew up without a father figure in their lives.

+ **The personal, one-on-one aspect of mentoring is something our society desperately needs.**

Judges who review presentencing investigative reports will tell you that the absence of a father or a positive male figure is a key indicator in the lives of the people they sentence to time in prison. We need strong men to build into the lives of our younger men and boys. Not extraordinary people; just ordinary, everyday men who care enough to invest themselves—their time, attention, and wisdom—in the lives of others, whether as a part of their natural leadership environment or as an additional relationship they purposefully undertake. We need people like that—men *and* women—to stem the tide of wasted lives and wasted potential that is increasing at an alarming rate across our nation.

Author Donald Miller founded a group he calls The Mentoring Project, with the not-so-modest goal to close 15 percent of U.S. prisons within a generation through an intentional development of mentoring relationships. Miller, who also serves on the presidential task force on promoting responsible fatherhood, agrees with me that fatherless young men, especially inner-city African Americans, are in desperate need of positive, involved role models. Government statistics show that one in three boys grows up without a father in the home—a statistic that rises to two out of three for African Americans.

Boys and girls without a father at home are five times more likely to end up in poverty and much more likely to make decisions that will negatively affect their lives far into the future, including criminal behavior, drug use, and teen pregnancy.

The need is clear and urgent for men who care about fatherless boys—who simply care whether they live or die and who care enough to pass along what it means to truly be a man.

> ✢ Part of our purpose in life is to build a legacy—a consistent pattern of building into the lives of others.

The same is true for young girls in our society. We need more women as well to step up as role models for young girls, women who will spend time with girls, affirming them and building into their lives what it means to be a woman of value, significance, and values. In developing relationships with young girls, these women will make an immediate and long-term difference in the girls' lives, helping them to become all that God created them to be.

The Mentoring Project's method has been to bring two existing entities together: the church and Big Brothers Big Sisters programs around the country. In most cities, Big Brothers Big Sisters has an extensive waiting list of kids in need of a "big brother" or "big sister." Most churches, meanwhile, have a willing population of people seeking a program to integrate into or a ministry opportunity where they can make a difference. The goal of The Mentoring Project is to quickly expand beyond its beginnings in Portland, Oregon (where Don Miller lives), and spread across the country through the existing network of Big Brothers Big Sisters, as churches awaken to the opportunity to serve.

Making a difference, through one-on-one mentoring relationships that truly embrace and demonstrate the value of a single life—that's what mentor leadership is all about.

Part of our purpose in life is to build a legacy—a consistent pattern of building into the lives of others with wisdom, experience, and loyalty that can then be passed on to succeeding generations. Think of the people in your own life whose legacy has touched you. Maybe it was a coach, a parent, a grandparent, or a teacher. It's a fact of our human existence that we need other people to live life with us—to walk alongside us and help us on the journey. That's one of the reasons why Derrick Brooks, a great linebacker who had a long career with the Tampa Bay Buccaneers, is so beloved in that city. He figured out that it wasn't enough to lend his name to programs for kids. He needed to get involved in the programs himself. He needed to go beyond providing tickets to football games; he needed to directly touch the lives of the kids who needed his help. Because Derrick Brooks is willing to "get his hands dirty" by going through life alongside a group of kids, the legacy he is building is tremendous—and inspiring.

+ **Building a life of significance, and creating a legacy of real value, means being willing to get your hands dirty.**

Building a life of significance, and creating a legacy of real value, means being willing to get your hands dirty. It means being willing to step out in your life and onto the platforms of influence you've been given and touch the lives of people in need. Whether it's in your business, your school, your community, or your family, if you want to make a difference in the lives of the people you lead, you must be willing to walk alongside them, to lift and encourage them, to share moments of understanding with them, and to spend time with them, not just shout down at them from on high.

Mentors build mentors.

Leaders build leaders.

When you look at it closely, it's really one and the same thing.

MENTOR LEADERS KEEP AN ETERNAL PERSPECTIVE

This Book of the Law shall not depart from your mouth, but you shall meditate on it day and night, so that you may be careful to do according to all that is written in it. For then you will make your way prosperous, and then you will have good success.

JOSHUA 1:8, ESV

The mentor leader sees time differently than other leaders. Though short-term results are important—there are upcoming games to prepare for or quarterly reports to complete or some other expectation placed on us—a leader must look into the distance, beyond the immediate return, where the rewards are more permanent, and where some rewards are eternal.

✢ **It takes time to build mentoring relationships. It takes time to add value to other people's lives.**

There is always a tension between demanding results *now* and implementing a longer-term perspective. In the National Football League, there are coaches and general managers who want to build a team that can win now, and others who gradually build a successful team. More often than not, coaches who try to build an immediate championship team end up mortgaging their future success at a great cost with free-agent acquisitions. Coaches who desire more sustainable, longer-term success will typically try to build their team through the draft. There's no guarantee that either way will work. Those competing tensions have blown up some good teams and good people when a middle ground could not be found.

Mentor leaders tend to lean toward longer-term results. They are involved in the present, but are willing to defer immediate gratification in order to build value and structure into people's lives, creating a culture based on something more than wins and losses. It takes time to build mentoring relationships. It takes time to add value to other people's lives and to achieve what the book of Joshua refers to as "good success." Here's how my good friend James Brown describes "good success" in his book *Role of a Lifetime: Reflections on Faith, Family, and Significant Living*:

> God's success is "good success." It's significance. It's making
> a difference in the lives of others. It's Joshua standing on the

banks of the Jordan River, feeling anxious and inadequate, and realizing that he is being called to do something that will make a difference in the lives of the people he is being called to lead. And in that moment, it's Joshua also realizing that he can only do it with the leadership and in the strength of God.*

Building an organization for "good success" means creating a culture that will live on through succeeding generations. It means building with a long-term perspective—a perspective that says when God is involved in the process, life takes on eternal significance.

The difficulty for most people is that maintaining a long-term perspective requires faith. For me, my faith in God directs, sustains, and strengthens my perspective on life and other people because I know that my true reward is eternal. By faith, I'm able to approach the events and circumstances of my life with an eternal perspective. Even though I may not see the results of my efforts today or even in my lifetime, I'm confident that doing the right thing—the *significant* thing—will yield rewards for the organization and for others far beyond what I might otherwise achieve.

+ **Building an organization for "good success" means creating a culture that will live on through succeeding generations.**

Every leader speaks of his or her own *vision*, but mentor leaders keep their eyes focused well downfield, understanding that many of the most significant moments and effects of their lives will happen outside of the public eye—possibly even outside of their own field of vision. In other words, they may never know the full impact of their leadership.

Mike Tomlin, the current head coach of the Pittsburgh Steelers,

*James Brown, *Role of a Lifetime* (New York: FaithWords, 2009), 101.

worked for me as a defensive backs coach with the Buccaneers. During his final season in Tampa, Mike coached a backup safety named Scott Frost. Scott never became a major NFL star, but he went on to a successful coaching career when his playing days were over. Whether Mike knew it or not, he had a significant impact on that young defensive back. Several years later, when Scott came to our house to recruit our son Eric for his college program, I could almost hear Mike speaking through Scott's words.

Mike Tomlin probably knows that he helped Scott Frost become a better player. What he might not know is how profoundly he affected the way Scott would coach hundreds of players during his coaching career. But I know that Eric Dungy will definitely be affected—in a very positive way—by the way Mike Tomlin coached Scott Frost.

During my coaching career, I always talked to my players about doing the right thing the right way. As I shared in *Quiet Strength*, I wasn't always certain I was getting through to some of the guys, including defensive end Regan Upshaw, who was known for his colorful personality. Years later, my family and I ran into Regan and his family when we all happened to be vacationing in Rome. After we had spoken for a few minutes, Regan told me that all the things I had tried to teach him about life were finally making sense.

✛ **Our talents and our treasures may pay dividends so far down the road we may never see the outcome.**

It may take time before the results of our leadership are fully known. Our talents and our treasures may pay dividends so far down the road we may never see the outcome. But with the faith that comes from doing the right thing at the right time in the right way, the mentor leader knows that the payoff will be great—and possibly eternal.

ACTION STEPS

1. Evaluate your integrity: Are your actions consistent with your words?

2. Evaluate your impact: Are you making lives better?

3. Evaluate your perspective: Do you see people as central to the mission of your organization? Or do you see them simply as the means—the fuel—to get your organization from here to there?

4. Evaluate your goals: Are you building relationships, or are you building a tower to climb to the top?

5. Mentor leaders see the opportunity to interact with people—and to build into their lives along the way—as part of the journey itself. How are you looking for ways to directly engage with and influence other people?

6. How does your leadership style need to change so that people will flourish and grow around you?

7. You can lead from a position of authority, but the most effective leaders lead as they build relationships of influence. What can you do to move from an authority-based model to an influence-based model?

8. Identify one person whom you can begin to mentor. Don't look too far or too hard. The opportunity is right in front of you—at work, in your family, or with a friend. Granted, it could be a special situation, outside of your everyday circles of influence, like my relationship with Michael Vick. But more than likely, the person is someone with whom you already have a relationship.

9. Visit The Mentoring Project's Web site (www.thementoringproject .org) and consider how you can get involved.

10. From your perspective, what is the difference between "success" and "good success"?

CHAPTER 2

THE MIND-SET OF A MENTOR LEADER: "IT'S NOT ABOUT ME"

The man answered, "'You must love the LORD your God with all your heart, all your soul, all your strength, and all your mind.' And, 'Love your neighbor as yourself.'"

LUKE 10:27

On many teams, the veteran players will share some things with the new players, but not everything. Of course, everyone knows that the team's goal is to win, but some of the guys are concerned that the new players might ultimately take their jobs. On some teams, it's understood that new players have to work their way up through the ranks and "earn" the respect of the veterans before they're given full status as teammates.

One of the ways we were able to maintain our success with the Colts was by integrating new players into the system as quickly as possible. That happened because of our great coaching staff, but also because our veteran players mentored younger players. It was easy for me as the head coach to say, "Watch these veteran players and do what they do. They'll teach you." And because our players wanted to win championships and be the best team they could be, they were willing to take on a mentoring role.

That mentality was instilled in the team over time. Most of the guys who are now veterans benefited from that type of mentoring when they were young players. And those who weren't mentored realized how it inhibited their progress—and ultimately, the progress of the team.

Every year, I would challenge the players to remember that our goal was to be the best team we could be, and that eventually we would need contributions from everyone. We saw the fruit of mentor leadership when we got to the Super Bowl. Nick Harper, our veteran defensive back, got hurt and couldn't finish the game. Young Kelvin Hayden went in for him and made the game-winning interception. Kelvin was prepared for that moment in part because Nick had spent time with him and helped him to be ready. That's the kind of chemistry great *teams* have.

It's not about me.

It's not about you.

It's about others.

The single most important factor that differentiates mentor leaders from other leaders in any setting is their outward focus on others. Because mentor leaders are committed to building value into the lives of other people, it seems natural that they would want to cast their influence as widely as possible by creating a culture of mentoring. Unfortunately, too many leaders operate from a paradigm that asks, "How will this better me or better my organization?" "How will this improve the bottom line?" "How will this improve my chances of a bonus, a raise, or a promotion?" It's not necessarily their fault that they think this way; the paradigm of self-advancement is one that most people in our society are familiar with, and it's the foundation on which most leadership instruction is built.

The mentor leader, by contrast, looks at how he or she can benefit others—which ultimately benefits the individual *and* the organization. Think about it. Even if you're the most fantastic leader in history, you can't do everything in your organization yourself. How much better would things be if you were building leaders who were building leaders who were building leaders? This principle of leader multiplication will reap great rewards.

+ **The mentor leader looks at how he or she can benefit others—which ultimately benefits the individual *and* the organization.**

If you were to ask Colts fans who the on-field leader of the team is, many would say Peyton Manning. Given that he's an All-Pro quarterback who leads the offense, it makes sense and is certainly true. But what I observed during my years with the Colts is that we became a much better team—and a much better organization—when other players on the fifty-three-man roster also stepped up alongside Peyton to take leadership responsibility.

Peyton Manning would be the first to tell you that his goal is not to be seen as the leader of the Colts. His goal is to win championships. Therefore, as Peyton leads the team in the huddle and on the field, he also educates and helps his teammates. He knows that the more leaders there are on the team, the better off he and the Colts will be.

I've also discovered, through my study of Scripture, that the mentoring mind-set can be seen in Jesus' interactions with others. If you think about how He spoke to His disciples, it's clear that Jesus was committed to making others better, equipping and enabling them to become mentor leaders themselves. Likewise, in His teaching, He modeled some of the central principles of mentoring. For example, in the Gospel of Luke, we find the story of a religious leader who came to Jesus and asked, "What should I do to inherit eternal life?" Jesus responded by asking the man what the law of Moses said. The man replied, "'You must love the LORD your God with all your heart, all your soul, all your strength, and all your mind.' And, 'Love your neighbor as yourself.'" The man was seeking an answer that would point him toward eternal life—for himself. But Jesus pointed him first toward God, then others. Jesus then told the parable of the Good Samaritan, which again illustrates the principle of putting the interests of others before our own—even at great personal cost.

✛ **When it comes to effective leadership, it's not about you and what makes you comfortable or helps you get ahead. It's about other people.**

So, when it comes to effective leadership, it's not about you and what makes you comfortable or helps you get ahead.

It's about other people. It's about serving God by serving others. That's the mind-set of the mentor leader.

THE FOCUS OF A MENTOR LEADER

For everything there is a season, a time for every activity under heaven. . . . A time to tear down and a time to build up. . . . A time to be quiet and a time to speak.

ECCLESIASTES 3:1, 3, 7

As we've seen, what differentiates the mentor leader from other types of leaders is *focus*. Mentor leaders realize that leadership is not about them. Instead, they look beyond themselves, focusing on the people they lead and where they should be going *together*. Over time, the result is that the people they lead are better able to handle all situations, even stressful ones, and the organization—team, business, church, or family—is better as well.

Too many people, when placed in positions of leadership, stay so focused on themselves that they are never able to step back and think about the people who are following them—the very people it is their responsibility to lead. Some, sadly, don't seem to care about those they lead.

I'm often disappointed when I read or hear about coaches who insist on their own system or on a top-down coaching style, or who feel that the only way they can effectively lead is through dictatorial or controlling methods of leadership.

That's too bad—in part because I don't think it's very effective. It's demoralizing, and when the team doesn't achieve its goal of winning—or, sadly, even when it does—it leaves everyone in the organization feeling empty. But it's also too bad because coaches who make winning the ultimate goal put pressure on themselves and others to win and win now. They don't give themselves the time, space, or opportunity to become the type of leaders who could begin to change lives, and their organizations, for the better and for the long term.

+ **Mentor leaders look beyond themselves, focusing on the people they lead and where they should be going together.**

Don't get me wrong: There are times when mentor leaders will do things differently depending on the circumstances or the level of experience of those we lead. Paul Hersey and Ken Blanchard pioneered an understanding of "situational leadership" when they were studying organizational behavior in the 1970s. Their research studies are straightforward and important to understand. Hersey and Blanchard discovered that different styles of leadership—telling, selling, participating, and delegating—are appropriate at different times, depending on the *audience* (those we lead) and the *situation*.

There are certain circumstances when we will have to mandate, dictate, and control because that's what the situation calls for. There will be times when, clearly, a more hands-on management style is required.

For example, during my first year as head coach in Tampa, we had a fan appreciation day, when we invited fans to come to the stadium, meet the players, and get autographs. It was a hot day, and after a while some of our veteran players left the field and went underneath the awnings and away from the crowd to escape the heat. They were content to let the younger players interact with the fans. I was at another part of the field signing autographs at the time and didn't see this happening. When it was brought to my attention, we were approaching a crisis—our team's behavior was turning off the very fans we were trying to win over.

As much as I view myself a teacher, we didn't have time at that point for a public relations lesson or a discussion about what was wrong with how we planned the event. In one of my few outbursts directed at the team, I used the stadium's public address system to announce that every player had better be on the field signing autographs or we would have some new players on the team that afternoon.

✛ **The audience in situational leadership will affect which style is appropriate at which time.**

They complied. After another hour of signing, with our fans now happy and some of our players now disgruntled, we went back to our offices, where I was able to discuss the situation with the players. I listened to their complaints and acknowledged that this event had been about sacrifice. It wasn't necessarily fun, but it was part of our plan and needed to be executed. I promised that the next year we would address some of their concerns—adding tents, cooling fans, and water.

The lesson I think our players learned that day was that I was sensitive to their concerns and would always listen to their side of things, but there would also be times when I would make a decision and they would simply have to march.

The audience in situational leadership will affect which style is appropriate at which time. That is, if the people we are leading are young and unskilled or immature in handling responsibility, they may not be capable of taking on as much leadership empowerment as we would like to give them at first. But even if we occasionally have to adjust our leadership style in light of temporary circumstances, our long-term focus should still be on building into the members of our organization so that in all situations they learn how to respond properly. If we will take the time to teach and equip them to handle adversity, success, and changing circumstances on their own,

> ✛ Our long-term focus should be on building into the members of our organization so that they learn how to respond properly.

and if we will give them the opportunity to develop and test their own judgment, then the time will come when we won't have to exercise moment-by-moment, hands-on control because we've already spent our time mentoring rather than directing.

Situational leadership means that different styles are appropriate at different times, and it is important that a leader be discerning enough and close enough to the situation to know when to use a particular style. But mentor leaders aren't satisfied with simply understanding when to apply the principles and styles of situational leadership. Rather, they are focused more on extending their influence through what the sports media love to call "the coaching tree"—that is, the ongoing progression of leaders building leaders who are equipped to build other leaders.

This aspect of mentor leadership, the "regenerative" aspect, is what sets it apart from other leadership paradigms. It's one thing to lead high-performing teams; it's quite another to lead high-performing teams that can perform at that level time and again and can also spawn other high-performing teams. The key to creating new generations of leaders is looking beyond yourself toward others—toward those you have been called to lead—and growing them into new leaders through intentional mentoring relationships. It's about *them*, not you.

Leadership that regenerates is what allows teams to win consistently. Frankly, people who can lead effectively for a time are a dime a dozen, in my opinion. People who understand basic leadership skills and are able to implement them are not unique. But leaders who are willing to place the focus somewhere other than on themselves are truly unique. That is precisely the mind-set and focus necessary for mentor leadership.

Before you jump on board, and before we go any further, you must ask yourself one question, the answer to which makes all the difference. When you get right down to it, mentor leadership may not be where you want to go. It sounds easy—building up other people; but for most of us, especially in a culture that has changed price tags on success, it's difficult to honestly and wholeheartedly internalize the core values of mentor leadership. It truly goes against everything we are taught by the culture in today's society.

✛ **Am I prepared to have great success and not get any credit for it?**

Take a moment to think about your answer to this question: *Am I prepared to have great success and not get any credit for it?*

Sure, if your business, your team, or your family does well, people will take notice—and they'll notice who the leader is. And you may be accorded some of the credit you feel you deserve. But if you do it right—if you really mentor others—more often than not, people will notice what a remarkably talented team, staff, or child you have rather than what a great coach, employer, or parent you are. They will assume that anyone could win with your team or family, and they'll say things like, "Just look at how well they work together. If I had selfless people like that, I could meet my quarterly goals as well."

I saw this very thing happen with Chuck Noll and the Pittsburgh Steelers. Coach Noll was an extraordinary leader and the catalyst of a team that won four Super Bowls in six years, but he was never voted Coach of the Year. Instead, people always pointed to the number of Hall of Fame–caliber players the Steelers had. But that's just the way Coach Noll wanted it—never having anyone guess that he might have been responsible for developing that talent.

As we move on with our discussion of mentor leadership, here's what you need to understand: If you do it right, as a mentor leader you may make it all but impossible for other people to give you credit.

Are you certain that you're okay with that?

If so, let's keep pushing forward.

> ✛ If you do it right, as a mentor leader you may make it all but impossible for other people to give you credit.

MAXIMIZING THE PRESENT WHILE ENVISIONING THE FUTURE

Have you ever danced in the rain
Or thanked the sun
Just for shining . . .
Take it all in
The world's a show

SISTER HAZEL, "CHANGE YOUR MIND"

A compelling vision and a clear mission statement are absolutely critical to effective leadership and a leader's ability to lead. However, in the process of planning and looking ahead, too many people lose sight of the present and forget to enjoy the journey along the way. For the mentor leader, though, life is about the destination *and* the journey.

How many times in the New Testament do we read about Jesus stopping along the way to tend to someone's immediate needs? Even while He was looking ahead to wherever He was traveling, He never lost sight of what was important right before His eyes in real time.

In Mark 10, Jesus stops to heal a blind man who is calling to Him from the side of the road, even while others are trying to move the man out of the way so he won't bother Jesus. In Luke 19, we see Jesus stop and ask Zacchaeus, a despised tax collector, to come down out of a tree—where he had climbed to get a better look at Jesus as He came down the road. Jesus knew that Zacchaeus felt life was empty and meaningless, so He invited Himself to a meal at the tax collector's house. In John 4, we watch as Jesus stops to help a Samaritan woman at a well in the heat of the day. Time and time again, through the example of His own life, Jesus reminds us that the present is where we need to spend our time in order to better the people around us and those along the way.

✢ **It's relatively easy in today's world to lose sight of the present in view of our goals and ambitions.**

All too often, we lose sight of those lessons from Jesus and focus so completely on the goals and outcomes we expect to see in the future—which are understandably important—that we cast all else aside in the headlong pursuit of them. How many people have you seen who have blindly pursued a path, only to realize that the ultimate cost was much higher than they anticipated?

It's relatively easy in today's world to lose sight of the present in view of our goals and ambitions. And it's relatively easy, as leaders, to become so focused on our destination that we don't allow ourselves or the members of our organization to enjoy the journey. After all, if we take our eyes off the goal, it could affect the bottom line. And often our job security is tied to the bottom line. So we point the team in an all-consuming sprint toward the outcome—the future—we are all trying to achieve.

Too many people climb the corporate ladder, striving to reach the top, only to get there and realize that there is nothing there. And then they look around and discover they are married to a stranger, living with children they don't know, and without the friends, hobbies, or other interests they never had a chance to nurture or develop while heeding the siren call of achievement.

Perhaps if we as leaders will take the time to push back, slow down, look around, and take stock of our priorities, we will find ourselves in a position to keep or—perhaps for the first time—put the other things of life in their proper places.

The first step, of course, is to understand and appreciate that the journey is as important as the destination. It's a little like playing golf—which I used to make time for many years ago, until I realized that a simple walk on the golf course would do a whole lot more for my nerves and confidence than trying to play that frustrating game. The added benefit was that I could take my wife and family with me on that walk.

> ✛ The first step is to understand and appreciate that the journey is as important as the destination.

I have noticed that too many golfers become so focused on the result of any given shot that they never enjoy the moment—before, during, or after the shot. I could see myself headed that way if I ever got good enough to even dream about recording a decent score. The problem with that laser-like approach to the game—get the ball in the hole at all costs—is that you miss the joy of the four- or five-hour journey along the way. You miss out on real fellowship with the others in your group, the very ones who have blessed you with their time and their presence. You miss the beauty of God's creation all around you and the beauty of the day. And because your ball just went into the pond near the green instead of rolling into the cup as you had envisioned, you probably missed seeing the mother duck swimming hurriedly along with her five ducklings close behind or the alligator sunning on the bank just out of reach.

A good friend of mine taught me the importance of enjoying the journey and not letting a vision for the future cloud my view of the present—a present, I might add, that we will never have the chance to live again.

Mike Mularkey played for the Pittsburgh Steelers and Minnesota Vikings before becoming an outstanding coach for a number of NFL teams. Several years ago, while he was still an assistant, he was offered an opportunity to become a head coach—which was his ultimate goal in coaching. When I heard about the offer sometime later—and how he had quietly and without a lot of fanfare turned down the job—I asked him why he had declined.

The story is one you don't see lived out much today. It goes against all that society preaches to us as the route to success. Mike's eldest son was about to enter his senior year of high school, and the Mularkeys decided they wanted him to be able to finish at the school where he had been for his first three years. Mike and his wife, Betsy, agreed that if Mike were to take the head coaching position, he would go alone and allow the family to stay in Pittsburgh until their son graduated. The offer was attractive, but the more Mike thought about it, the more uncomfortable he became with the idea of a 300-mile commute and the time away from his family that the distance would create. He knew that the long hours and the demands of an NFL training camp and season would limit his trips home.

He had witnessed a similar scenario a few years earlier, when the Steelers had hired an assistant coach from the Seahawks. This coach had left his family behind in Seattle, where they planned to stay for a year before joining him in Pittsburgh. However, almost immediately after he took the job with the Steelers, the coach's wife was diagnosed with an advanced stage of cancer. She needed to stay in Seattle for treatment, and he visited whenever he could, but not nearly as much as he wanted. She died within months of the diagnosis, and as a result, he missed both the quantity and quality of time he and she should have had in her last days. Sometimes tomorrow never comes.

After weighing the costs, Mike declined the head coaching

position. "Other people have to commute all the time," he said. "But we didn't have to. My family didn't need for me to be an NFL head coach—if I'd taken the job, it would have been about me." As the leader of his family, he realized that his decision needed to be about them. So he passed on the opportunity.

There are only thirty-two head coaching positions in the National Football League, and there is no shortage of candidates for the few vacancies that occur each year. Mike actually became a head coach a couple of years later, with the Buffalo Bills; but at the time he made his initial decision, there was no guarantee he would ever get a second chance, and he knew that. For some, taking the job, the separation from family, and the commute might have been the right answer. For Mike, it wasn't the right time.

This is not a commentary on commuting. I actually commuted for two seasons in Indianapolis, my first and my last. As my dad had done when he changed jobs while I was in high school, my wife Lauren and I prayed about it and decided that preserving continuity for our kids and their schooling would take precedence for the short term over my physical presence each day.

This is true for many other families as well, especially in these tough economic times, when people may not be able to be as selective about their working conditions or locations. This is not intended to make you feel guilty or to suggest that you should do otherwise—again, I did it by choice. Instead, this is a reminder that we all must count the costs and make our decisions as congruent with our priorities as possible.

✦ **We all must count the costs and make our decisions as congruent with our priorities as possible.**

For Mike, based on his priorities and where he was in life, it wasn't the right decision. He knew and appreciated that the present was just as important a part of his life—and his family's lives—as the future.

Enjoy the journey—especially today, because the future you envision may never come.

VISION, MISSION, AND VALUES

Leadership is the art of getting someone else to do something you want done because he wants to do it.

DWIGHT D. EISENHOWER

The vision, mission, and values we establish in life are the guiding lights for our lives and the lives of those we lead. Those three elements create the "goalposts" for the decisions and actions of our lives. They should direct and guide everything we do—and we should develop them prayerfully as we move forward.

Vision

Much has been written about the importance of vision—and for good reason. The best leaders throughout history—like Dwight Eisenhower—have been people who were able to articulate a vision that was simple, clear, and compelling.

Mentor leaders cast a vision well beyond themselves and their own interests. Vision paints the picture of where we want to be, what we want to look like, what we hope things will be like in the future if we do what we feel we are called to do as a team or an organization. A well-cast vision is one that can be commonly shared by all members of the team and that all team members can—and must—buy into. In order for the vision to be compelling, however, it must encompass more than merely the leader's best interests; it must include goals and benefits that resonate with the entire team. It must be something they can see and believe is possible to achieve

✣ **A well-cast vision is one that can be commonly shared by all members of the team.**

with their collective efforts. In order to generate enthusiasm and excitement, the vision must be something larger than any one individual, larger even than the sum of the members of the team, and team members must see it as something worth achieving.

At times the leaders are the only ones in a position to fully see down the line to what they have envisioned. Their job is to continually direct the other members of the team to share that vision. They must continually set out the vision as a beacon to both guide and invigorate the team members, to keep them from quitting before the dawn of fulfillment arrives.

Younger readers may not realize that Troy Polamalu, who starred in the Coke Zero ads aired during Super Bowl XLIII, isn't the original Steelers pitchman for Coca-Cola. In fact, those ads are actually a spoof of an unforgettable Coke commercial from 1979 starring Mean Joe Greene, the Steelers' Hall of Fame defensive tackle.

Joe was one of my teammates with the Steelers, and he told me one time how close he had come to never making it to any Super Bowls. I was a young rookie at the time, hanging on the great Joe Greene's every word, amazed that he might have been a nonfactor in the Steelers' incredible success during the 1970s—though I had no doubt they would not have achieved that level of success without him. Joe shared his story with me, and with others, because he wanted us to know that we should never quit—because you never know when things might turn around. But more than that, his story demonstrates the importance of understanding, believing, and buying into the vision of the team or organization of which you are a part. It's a story I shared often with my teams in Tampa and Indianapolis.

No doubt you've heard the saying, "It's always darkest just before the dawn." What makes it that way, I think, is that we usually aren't able to tell when dawn is about to break through. Joe Greene wondered how many people walk away just before the break of dawn—like he almost did. He was fortunate, however, because he received a second chance to become a part of the dawning of the Steelers dynasty of the 1970s.

In 1969, Joe was drafted out of North Texas State (now the University of North Texas) with the fourth pick of the first round of the NFL draft. During his first season, the Steelers won their first game and then proceeded to lose the next thirteen. They headed into 1970, which was also Chuck Noll's second year as head coach, with a quarterback they had drafted in the first round—Terry Bradshaw. That year, they improved to five wins and nine losses. In 1971, the third season for both Coach Noll and Joe Greene, they finished with six wins and eight losses. In retrospect, it's clear to see the trend line was moving in the right direction, but Joe was sick and tired of losing. He continued to hear Coach Noll say that they were improving as a team, even though they weren't seeing the results they hoped to see on the scoreboard. They were also improving the level of talent on the team, and the team was gaining a better understanding of Coach Noll's system. But without the level of winning that Joe expected at this point in his career, he was increasingly having trouble buying in.

Each year, they continued to add more talent, including future Hall of Fame defenders Mel Blount and Jack Ham, to go with Bradshaw and Greene. When they selected Penn State fullback Franco Harris in the first round of the 1972 draft, Joe expected to see some appreciable improvement on the field. But when the season opened with two wins and two losses, it seemed the team was once again headed for mediocrity.

The night after the second loss, Joe watched the Miami Dolphins, a great team that was on its way to an undefeated season, play on *Monday Night Football. This is what a football team should look like,* he thought.

The next morning, Joe walked into Three Rivers Stadium, cleaned out his locker, and headed to the airport. Word got back to Coach Noll that Mean Joe Greene had left the building, and the assumption was that he was done with the Steeler Way.

Coach Noll calmly sent assistant coach Lionel Taylor to find Joe at the airport. As Joe tells the story, Coach Noll said, "Lionel, Joe is thinking about giving it up. You may want to head to the airport and see if you can find him." Of course Chuck was calm; he believed every player was "important but not indispensable."

When Lionel tracked Joe down at the airport, Joe vented his frustration about the team. He said he didn't think they would ever start playing well in Pittsburgh and that they would never look like the Dolphins had looked the night before.

Whatever Lionel told Joe, it was enough to get him to leave the airport and return home to think through his decision a little more. As Joe told me, if he'd left for Texas, he *might* have ultimately come back to Pittsburgh—but it was just as likely that he never would have returned.

But he showed up for practice the next day, which happened to coincide with the coaching staff's decision to give Franco Harris an increased role in the offense. Up to then, Franco hadn't played much. It turned out to be just the spark the team needed. The Steelers went on to win nine of their next ten games to finish the regular season at 11–3. They then faced the Oakland Raiders in the opening game of the playoffs, in a game that came to be known as "The Immaculate Reception" game because of the game-winning catch made by none other than Franco Harris, who snatched a deflected pass off his shoe-tops and ran it into the end zone.

The next week, the Steelers played the Dolphins in the AFC Championship Game for the right to go to Super Bowl VII. The Dolphins won, 21–17, on their way to that perfect season. However, the Steelers' run to accomplish what they had set out to accomplish had begun, and the team would go on to win Super Bowls in 1974,

1975, 1978, and 1979. And Joe Greene was an integral part of all of those teams.

Joe's story is ultimately a story of success, but it also illustrates one of the challenges of mentor leadership: Not everyone is going to embrace the vision or have the patience and belief in the vision to conclude the process. Sometimes, within an organization, the tide seems to be rolling the other way—especially when circumstances seem bleak.

✢ **Keep the vision out front. Don't let your team—wherever it is—quit early.**

The apostle Paul must have felt that way at times. When he was imprisoned, whipped, shipwrecked, stoned, or told to leave a city, he must have thought, *There is no way this new movement is going to end well.* But guided by the vision imparted to him by Jesus Christ, Paul pressed on toward the goal. Thank goodness he did, because Paul was an integral part of God's vision to advance His Kingdom, and he did much to advance the gospel, including writing major sections of the New Testament that many of us turn to today for guidance, inspiration, and hope during our own times of shipwreck or failure.

The mentor leader's job is to continue to cast the vision, to remind everyone in the organization of their common goals, and to give people an inspirational hook to hang on to so they won't be tempted to give up when times get tough. Preserving the vision will sometimes depend entirely on faith—the hope of things not yet seen. At other times, we may have some objective evidence, no matter how small or incremental, that shows progress and thus keeps us moving forward. Leaders must use their best judgment to determine the best approach.

Keep the vision out front. Don't let your team—wherever it is—quit early.

And don't you quit, either.

Mission

A mission statement—whether it's for an organization, institution, family, team, or individual—serves to answer a fundamental question: Why do we exist?

In other words, why are we doing what we're doing? Why bother with all of this, anyway?

One worthy piece of advice I've run across comes from Patrick Lencioni, the noted author of *The Five Dysfunctions of a Team*. In his book for families, *The Three Big Questions for a Frantic Family*, Lencioni suggests that while it is absolutely critical to cast a vision, develop a worthy mission, and take note of your values, too often people get jammed up in the planning process and don't make much progress. Some people are steeped in the technical aspects of business and leadership, and they already think in terms of vision, mission, and values; but if you're not one of those people, Lencioni suggests that you simply craft a mission to the best of your ability, encapsulating the items that make your family or team unique, and then run with it.

+ Craft a mission to the best of your ability, encapsulating the items that make your family or team unique, and then run with it.

Many people get hung up wondering whether they've embedded the proper values in their mission statements or feeling as if their missions aren't comprehensive enough. They study them, ask others about them, rewrite them, and then do it all over again—and they never actually move ahead with their missions.

Don't get caught up in the paralysis of analysis. Go! Do! Act! Over time, if you realize that your mission statement is slightly off, you can revise it. But first start moving forward; put your mission into action.

Vision and mission are dynamic components of the direction God wants us to go. They will change over time as we are guided by God's Word and by the disciplines of our faith amid the changing needs in our society. If God wants us to retool, redevelop, or redirect our efforts, He will guide us in those new directions. If we have trouble hearing Him, He will faithfully work in our lives until we are pointed in the direction He wants us to go.

First cast the vision. Then establish the mission. Then get moving!

Values

The final component that guides any sound organization is its values. Values, very simply, can be thought of as the "rules of the road." They tell us and others what is important to us—as leaders, as an organization, and as individuals. They are the rudder that steers the ship. They tell us how to treat other people, both inside and outside the team or organization.

+ Values tell us and others what is important to us— as leaders, as an organization, and as individuals.

The values we adopt as leaders will paint a picture for others that is appealing and attractive, of someone they want to be associated with—or not. Our values will determine how we as leaders approach, care for, and develop our mentoring relationships.

Taken as a whole, our vision, mission, and values tell the world who we are, what is important to us, and what guides our lives. They're a snapshot of who we are and of the type of leaders we will be.

For mentor leaders, our values will clearly demonstrate that we are committed to the advancement and well-being of other people—those we are called to serve and lead.

IT'S ALL ABOUT SERVING

For even the Son of Man came not to be served but to serve others and to give his life as a ransom for many.

MARK 10:45

For me, leadership has always been about service. Much has been said and written about service, or servant leadership, based on the model that Jesus provided during His ministry.

The principal focus of service-directed leadership must be on a point beyond ourselves. Such leadership must be *other* directed and *other* inspired. Mentor leadership must be grounded in and springing from an emphasis on *service* as its primary focus. Mentor leaders desire to help those they are privileged to lead to be better in whatever roles and responsibilities they have. Truly serving others requires putting ourselves and our desires aside while looking for ways and opportunities to do what is best for others.

> ✛ Truly serving others requires putting ourselves and our desires aside while looking for ways and opportunities to do what is best for others.

Don't get me wrong; it's not easy. Not only that, but it runs contrary to the prevailing wisdom of the world, which focuses on personal success, achievement, and advancement. We live in a world that insists on "looking out for number one." We're encouraged to ask, "What's in it for me?" and, "What have you done for me lately?" After all, if you don't make sure you get the credit, who will? And if you don't get the credit, how will you ever get that raise or promotion? Who will ever recognize you for a job well done?

One of the great object lessons in the Bible is found in John 13:3-8, right before the Last Supper, when Jesus washes the feet of His disciples:

Jesus knew that the Father had given him authority over everything and that he had come from God and would return to God. So he got up from the table, took off his robe, wrapped a towel around his waist, and poured water into a basin. Then he began to wash the disciples' feet, drying them with the towel he had around him.

When Jesus came to Simon Peter, Peter said to him, "Lord, are you going to wash my feet?"

Jesus replied, "You don't understand now what I am doing, but someday you will."

"No," Peter protested, "you will never ever wash my feet!"

Jesus replied, "Unless I wash you, you won't belong to me."

The roads in those days were unpaved, and because people wore open sandals, their feet were normally covered with dust, dirt, or mud. Most households kept large basins of water at the door, and a servant of the house was usually there with towels and cleaning tools to wash the soiled feet of guests before they came in.

But on the night of the Last Supper, for whatever reason, there were no servants to perform this cleansing ritual. The disciples probably should have shared the foot-washing duties among themselves, but they were so caught up with personal and professional pride, trying to determine who deserved a place of honor at the table and in the hierarchy of God's Kingdom, that none of them bothered to accept the responsibility. Instead, Jesus did what He so often did: He used the moment to teach His disciples an important lesson about leadership. It was a lesson He had been trying to teach them, and now He had the perfect opportunity to get His point across. He took the towels and the water and began to wash their feet.

He did what the servant was expected to do.

Peter, one of Jesus' closest friends, objected. Perhaps it was because he felt that Jesus shouldn't be the one to do this. Maybe. But notice that Peter hadn't stepped up to do it either, which gives us some additional insight. I think Peter knew that Jesus was setting the bar for the disciples—that what He was doing was what He expected Peter and the other disciples to do for other people. He was trying to change their mind-set—their attitude—to one of service.

Wash their feet.

Serve them.

Share the Good News.

If Peter was to continue to be one of Jesus' disciples, one of His chosen leaders to carry the message to others, he needed to be willing to humble himself and serve others—a lesson he was now learning firsthand from the King of kings, who was kneeling before Peter wiping the filthy grime off his feet.

In our culture, what Jesus was doing would not be seen as a pathway to promotion or credit. Yet it's the very path a mentor leader must take. Humble servant leadership demonstrates to those you lead that you see them as valuable, and it's worth your time to serve them—not to have them serving you. It's a path that flips the world's model upside down: leaders who serve—not just when it's convenient, neat, and acceptable,

> ✢ Servant leadership flips the world's model upside down: leaders who serve— not just when it's convenient, neat, and acceptable, but when it's timely, needed, and right.

but when it's timely, needed, and right. Jesus, through His actions, showed us that servant leadership isn't theoretical lip service. Instead, it's hands-on, get-yourself-dirty, humble service. In our day and age, with paved streets and closed-toe shoes, foot washing is no longer necessary. But the principle is still valid.

What can you do in your organization to "wash the feet" of the people you lead?

What do you suppose they would do after that experience?

Logic would indicate that they just might do the same for others. And those others for still others. And so on.

Now we're off and running.

If you can make the leap from traditional leadership models to one that believes that the people you lead are worthy of your time and service and that educating, equipping, and empowering them is crucial to your ultimate success, it will change the dynamic of your organization—*completely*.

Taken a step further, intentional, direct service to others—in a word, *mentoring*—is the key to leadership success on a consistent, long-term basis. That's because people who are served in this way tend to, by that example, serve others. Mentors produce mentors. Mentor leaders produce mentor leaders. And organizations that continue to build leaders in that fashion—with leaders who actively seek to mentor those around them—are the ones that historically sustain their position for the long term.

+ **Mentor leaders produce mentor leaders.**

I sometimes picture mentor leadership as an inverted organizational chart. Typically, an organizational chart will have the number one person, or the board, at the top, with subordinates (even the name doesn't sound inviting) in levels of reporting and supervisory responsibility below. The natural effect of this display is to create a desire in everyone to be at the top of the diagram—at the pinnacle of his or her profession.

Now, instead of the usual diagram, picture the chart with the number one leader at the bottom and the lines of responsibility and reporting spreading upward and outward. Think about each "subordinate" role now as a position of lifter, equipper, and encourager to the ones above it on the chart. It certainly looks more precarious this way, rather than the usual model where each level drops down passively from the line above. Precarious, I suppose, because at any moment, if one of the people below stopped lifting the ones above, the whole chart could begin to crumble and fall. But when the leaders below accept their responsibility to lift, equip, and encourage the people above them—and when this attitude pervades the organization—what once seemed precarious now looks connected, supportive, and balanced.

When viewed this way, with the leader having the responsibility to help, support, and encourage everyone else, it changes everyone's outlook. And when everyone else understands that his or her role is also to lift, encourage, and equip—and that all members of the organization are dependent on one another—it becomes clear that nurturing relationships is necessary to the organization's health. Now those roles within the organization move from being positions of authority to positions of *influence*—or, dare I say, positions of service?

ACTION STEPS

1. Evaluate your focus: Is it centered on benefiting others?

2. Evaluate your influence: Are you focused on developing your "coaching tree"—building leaders who build leaders, generation after generation?

3. Evaluate your audience: Are you able to preserve a long-term focus on growing others while at times appropriately exercising more direct control and involvement?

4. Look ahead: Know your vision, mission, and values, but remember that life is about the journey, too.

5. Focus on the present: What can you do *today* to build into the lives of the people around you? Don't miss the *now*. Remember, tomorrow may never come.

6. Evaluate your vision: What do you hope the future will look like as you proceed?

7. Evaluate your personal and organizational mission: Does it clearly tell you and the world what you're about, why you're here, and why you have chosen these goals?

8. Evaluate your values: Are your "rules of behavior" consistent with your principles? Does your "rudder" steer you in a good direction for how you will behave and treat others?

9. Evaluate your approach with your family, team, business, friends, and others: Mentoring is a lifestyle.

10. Remember that mentor leadership is all about serving. Jesus said, "For even the Son of Man came not to be served but to serve others and to give his life as a ransom for many" (Mark 10:45).

CHAPTER 3

THE MATURITY OF A MENTOR LEADER: A LOOK WITHIN

The unexamined life is not worth living.

SOCRATES

In order to become an effective mentor leader, in whatever setting, it is important to take a look inside yourself. Identify what drives and motivates you, the areas in which you're naturally gifted, and the areas that are more challenging and thus will take more self-application to conquer. The ability to take an honest look at yourself and examine who you are—what makes you tick, what makes you do the things you do—is a mark of maturity for a mentor leader.

I know, in my own life, such periods of self-examination are not necessarily times I relish. Often they come about at the suggestion of another person—such as my wife, Lauren—when I am struggling through a difficult time or under pressure to make a decision. Ideally, though, this self-examination should be more intentional and regular, not just dictated by the demands of a particular moment.

In everything we do, our desire should be to honor God by actively seeking to become more like the people He wants us to be.

For men in particular, looking inside ourselves is not necessarily the easiest journey or one we readily volunteer to take. But it is essential throughout our lives if we want to continue to grow into all we are meant to be. As Coach Noll pointed out to me, every player loves to work on his strengths, but only the great ones work on their weaknesses. Coming to grips with our strengths *and* our weaknesses is essential to our roles as leaders—and as mentor leaders, in particular—if we hope to have a positive impact to mentor and lead others.

> ✛ A personal inventory can help you understand and evaluate the things that make you tick.

We are each uniquely and wonderfully made, different in so many ways. Yet we're each the sum total of the way we were raised, our cumulative experiences, and the environments to which we have been exposed. For better or worse, where we've been and who we've encountered along the way have shaped us and affected our perception of leadership and life. Some people stand on the shoulders of encouraging mentors they've had, whether they were coaches, teachers, or parents, whereas others must overcome the stings of defeat or the biting criticism they've received along the way. Still others may be on the verge of giving up. Even the most fortunate among us have challenges in life to overcome, and sometimes we choose ways of adapting that are not healthy, productive, or in line with God's plan for our lives.

A personal inventory can help you understand and evaluate the things that make you tick—that is, what makes you think, react, and respond the way you do, and what makes you do the things you do. In order to be effective mentor leaders, we must operate within the framework of a healthy self-awareness. What isn't good for us in our own lives should not be transmitted into the lives of others—children, spouses, team, staff, or employees. An honest, introspective self-evaluation will help us avoid transferring negative behaviors and attitudes to other people. At the same time, it will help us become the kind of people God wants us to be.

+ **The continued willingness to examine our own lives is an essential part of becoming the mentors that God wants us to be.**

The continued willingness to examine our own lives is an essential part of becoming the mentors that God wants us to be, the best mentor leaders we can be—destined to have the biggest possible impact on the people around us.

DEALING WITH THE PAST

Not everything that is faced can be changed. But nothing can be changed until it is faced.

JAMES BALDWIN

No one has a perfect past. I wish we all did, but we don't. Through a combination of circumstances, the decisions and actions of others, and our own decisions, both good and bad, we have arrived where we are today. Mature individuals are people who can examine their past honestly and understand how it affects them today. A careful look at where you have been and an understanding of how your past influences your decisions and direction in life can yield significant insights as you look ahead and seek to lead and mentor others.

I recognize that I grew up with certain advantages, compared to many kids today. I had the blessing of a wonderful family, with two loving parents who provided me with sound guidance well into my adult life. In fact, their steady and positive influence still guides me and the decisions I make and the type of impact I try to have with others. I had the good fortune to be raised with great siblings—a brother and two sisters—all three of whom have grown up to also have successful careers and influence in the lives of many people around them. I grew up with an abundance of aunts, uncles, and many others around me who always felt it was their responsibility to build positive character into me. Throughout my career, I've been surrounded by patient mentors, and I have had a supportive, loyal wife as a helpmate on the journey.

But it hasn't all been smooth. God doesn't promise that life will be easy, but He has promised that, no matter where we've been or what we've been through, He will never leave us. In the most difficult of times, these words of David from Psalm 23 still ring true for us today:

> The LORD is my shepherd;
>   I have all that I need. . . .
>   He renews my strength. . . .
> Even when I walk
>   through the darkest valley,
> I will not be afraid,
>   for you are close beside me. . . .
> Surely your goodness and unfailing love will pursue me
>   all the days of my life,
> and I will live in the house of the LORD
>   forever.

I suppose you might feel as if all you ever do, day after day, is get out of the frying pan only to find yourself in the middle of the fire. Life can be like that—even more so when you are carrying baggage from the past that continues to direct your decisions and actions today. Bags full of things you've done for which you can't forgive yourself. Bags stuffed with things that have been done to you—things for which you haven't forgiven others, things that have been said or done through the years that you began to see as defining who you are. Maybe someone called you names or characterized some of your habits, mannerisms, or physical attributes in a negative light, and you began to believe this person's view of you or at least to see yourself in a much dimmer light than the one God was trying to shine on you. Perhaps you were fired from a position and to this day that perceived failure affects your confidence. Maybe those who were supposed to care for you—parents, grandparents, foster parents, and others—didn't. Maybe they neglected you, hurt you, or abandoned you. The bags are full and getting harder and harder to carry with each step. With the weight of the past on your shoulders, it's difficult, if not impossible, to move forward and reach the place God has for you.

A person who carries emotional baggage through life is not much different from the person who refuses to check any bags at the airport. You've seen them—struggling with all kinds of carry-ons that you just know are not going to fit in the overhead bins. Sure, no one wants to check bags, but checking them makes it so much easier and smoother to get through the airport. Likewise with emotional baggage and life. Don't continue to struggle with baggage that only weighs you down and hinders your progress. Get help if you need it. Let God take the weight off your shoulders. He'll be happy to relieve you of that burden.

> ✛ Don't continue to struggle with baggage that only weighs you down and hinders your progress. Get help if you need it.

FORGIVENESS AND FREEDOM

Unloving people are unloved people. The people who are hurting you are hurting themselves. Hurt people hurt people.
KEN WHITTEN

Forgiving other people is difficult. Forgiving ourselves is sometimes even harder. But the ability to forgive—and to ask for forgiveness when we've hurt or offended someone else—is crucial to understanding what it is that makes us tick.

Forgiveness is not the easiest of godly attributes to embrace. But it might be the best medicine available to help you to get beyond things from the past that hold you down and keep you from achieving your godly potential. I suspect you'd be surprised if you saw a list of all the stuff other people had said or done to me that I carried around with me for far too long—well, I *hope* you'd be surprised. If you carry emotional baggage, the only person it bothers, affects, and holds back is *you*. So, before you take another step with all those grudges and hard feelings weighing you down, you might do well to remember God's promise in Jeremiah 31:34: "I will forgive their wickedness, and I will never again remember their sins."

✢ **If you carry emotional baggage, the only person it bothers, affects, and holds back is *you*.**

If God can forgive and forget all the things you've thought, said, and done in your life, shouldn't you be willing to forgive yourself and forgive other people? That's what God's grace—His unmerited love—is all about. Who in your life do you need to forgive or ask forgiveness of? What's holding you back? What in your life do you need to forgive yourself for? God's grace provides a way.

If you're like most people, you may want to move past a failure or offense and forgive yourself or someone else, but then something reminds you of that moment long ago, the bitterness or guilt returns, and that same old tight knot begins to form in the pit of your stomach again. It's emotional scar tissue or residual pain from a wound that may run deep within your emotional or mental makeup. Those old and deep wounds can affect us on a daily basis, often without our even knowing it is happening.

Sometimes the wounds may be so deep that we need the help and guidance of a trusted friend, a pastor, or a professional counselor to get to a place of healing. But we must pursue that healing before we can move forward with life in a healthy and productive way, let alone lead and nurture other people.

The baggage of guilt, heartache, anger, bad times, or deep pain from the past is no respecter of wealth or poverty; gender, race, ethnicity, or culture; age, IQ, or education. It cuts across all would-be divides and differences. And it keeps us from becoming all we were created to be. It not only keeps us from believing in ourselves, but it also prevents us from realizing that God believes in us. As potential leaders, if we ourselves are not empowered—if we don't believe in ourselves—it won't be long before we run out of make-believe energy as we try to empower and equip others to become the best they can be.

Of course, not everyone carries the same amount of baggage. But whether your wounds are deep or not, it is worth thinking through and facing the truth about your past, for it is what has brought you to where you are. The events and circumstances of your past—good, bad, or indifferent—are what have helped to create the person you are today. Your past has helped to set a course for what motivates, directs, and drives you, or what holds you back. It may be painful to face your past, but doing it will help you resolve the negative feelings you hold inside and get to a place where you remember—and cherish—that you are unique and that God loves you. The God who created you as a complex, emotional being has emotions and feelings of His own. He may even have shed some tears as He watched your early life unfold. But just as He forgives us for our sins and doesn't hold them against us, He also desires that we walk in freedom from the chains of our past. And that's what gives us hope.

+ **Your past has helped to set a course for what motivates, directs, and drives you, or what holds you back.**

Something or someone along the way may have slowed or hindered your progress, but your life is not over yet. God's design for you isn't fully completed, isn't fully realized yet. Likewise, as long as you have breath, God's purpose for your life is not yet finished. He has so much more for you to do. So let me encourage you to face what you need to face. Face what you have done or what has been done to you. Face who you are. Forgive and seek forgiveness. Get help if you need to. And then move on to become all that God intended for you to be, doing all that He intended for you to do.

Over the last ten years, Lauren and I have adopted four children. One of the beauties of continuing to adopt is that it has kept me young—reading books and watching movies designed for that younger audience. Through the experience of parenting, I have come to realize that the stories and principles of Hans Christian Andersen, the Brothers Grimm, Dr. Seuss, and Eric Carle are timeless and have lessons for all audiences.

Disney's *The Lion King* is one of our family favorites. We saw the Broadway production in Indianapolis, and it has a message that will resonate with audiences of any age. As the story opens, Simba, a newborn lion cub, is held aloft by Rafiki, a wise old baboon and seeming spiritual leader, signifying that Simba is the rightful heir to the throne—the next lion king—who will succeed his father, Mufasa, one day in the future.

✦ **As long as you have breath, God's purpose for your life is not yet finished. He has so much more for you to do.**

Mufasa invests time with Simba, teaching him what being heir to the throne means—who he is as a child of the king, and who he shall become. The king teaches his son about the vastness of the kingdom he will one day rule—as far as the eye can see. Yet, before Mufasa has time to make sure those lessons have firmly taken hold in his son's heart, he is killed while trying to save Simba from a stampede. Simba, believing his father's death is his fault, runs away from the guilt and shame he feels. He refuses to face what has happened, and in that, he abandons his birthright.

Life, as it does to many of us at times, has beaten him down, and he runs from all he was meant to be, from his future, with all the values, responsibilities, and life-changing power that would be his as the next lion king. Over time, he forgets.

All the progress he had made under his father's teaching, toward becoming the leader he was intended to be, has been thwarted by the guilt he now feels over his father's death.

But then, in an unexpected encounter with Rafiki in the wilderness, Simba is forced to face who he is. Looking at his reflection in a pond, he sees not only his own image but his father's—his past and his heritage. He is forced to remember where he has come from, what has happened, who he is, and who he should be. In that moment, he comes face-to-face with his past as well as his future. And he begins to step out again on the road to becoming all that he was created to be. When Simba is able to confront his past and forgive himself for what has occurred, he is able to return to his rightful place as the lion king.

Becoming what we are meant to be is a journey worth taking—for all of us. It's a journey that will free us from the hold of the past. It's a journey that will empower us for roles in the lives of others, as mentors, to help them become all that they were meant to be—under God's direction, guidance, encouragement, and grace, all along the way.

MOTIVATIONS, PRIORITIES, AND BALANCE

In the long run, men hit only what they aim at.
HENRY DAVID THOREAU

A mature leader can take an objective look in the mirror. Are there things that come easily to you? What are your greatest challenges? Are there things that excite you each day? What gets you out of bed in the morning? What are you afraid of?

The answers to those questions are different for each of us, but they may lead us to a greater understanding of what drives us.

We had a young man on our staff with the Buccaneers whose work ethic was beyond passionate. He worked coach's hours, making sure he was there almost every hour of the day, it seemed. And coach's hours are no laughing matter. As the head coach in Tampa and Indianapolis, I tried to set a family friendly work schedule, but the in-season hours were still daunting—Mondays and Tuesdays until late at night, and Wednesdays and Thursdays until eight or nine o'clock. Fridays we went home in the afternoon, but then it was back to work on Saturdays and Sundays—and throw in travel all weekend if it was a road game.

I appreciated this young man's commitment to the team. The only problem? He wasn't a coach. He worked in the front office, where hours were longer in the *off*-season, not during the season. Others in the front office worked less during the season, when there was less for them to do, to balance out the off-season, when their responsibilities increased dramatically. But he had created for himself the worst of both worlds—a lifestyle also shared by his family. Unfortunately.

He actually did a great job of trying to find time with his family, having them come to the office regularly to watch practice or eat meals with him, as did many others on our staff. But he was missing opportunities, for no good reason that I could figure out, to be with them in their world, on their time and schedule. But he just couldn't bring himself to leave the office while the coaches were still around, despite being told repeatedly by his supervisor, and by me, to go home earlier. He would always come up with a reason why he needed to stick around.

Finally, one day while we were talking, it dawned on me. He was a coach's son. He had clearly received the message as a youngster that *this is what it looks like to support your family*, and similarly, *this is what a football job requires.*

Of course, because he had viewed events with a child's eyes, what he didn't take into account was the downtime his father had during the off-season, which he himself didn't have. As a result, he wasn't giving his own family that flexibility now. For him, it wasn't a matter of priorities so much as it was a matter of understanding his motivation. His family and faith were important to him, and he spent his nonwork hours immersed in both. However, it wasn't until he realized that he was driven by his image of what a successful man was—the image through a child's eyes—that he was able to start making some positive changes.

Of course, those changes didn't come overnight. Ten years later, he says he has improved—and most of his coworkers would agree—but deep-seated motivations don't always cure themselves instantly. If it took a lifetime for you to get this way, it may take a little time to understand and reverse the negative effects.

> ✢ If it took a lifetime for you to get this way, it may take a little time to understand and reverse the negative effects.

Priorities are related to each other and to the limited time into which they must be squeezed. Devoting more time to one priority naturally limits the time available for something else. Acknowledging that life requires trade-offs at times and prioritizing the various aspects of our lives into the hours available each day provides us a road map to make decisions when those trade-offs become necessary. Doing this can also show us what we view as important at that particular time.

Over the last few years, I've gotten to know Urban Meyer, head coach of the University of Florida football team, and I really enjoy talking with him. He's a fantastic football coach, as his record and reputation indicate, but he has recently lived out a very public dialogue about priorities and balance in his personal and professional life.

On December 26, 2009, a week before his team's Sugar Bowl appearance, Urban unexpectedly resigned as head coach—effective after the bowl game—citing health issues and a desire to spend more time with his family as reasons for walking away. The following day, however, he adjusted course and announced a leave of absence instead, obviously torn between his priorities and his passions—none of which, including football, were bad in and of themselves.

This battle is one that is waged all the time by people who don't get the media attention but have the same struggle: passion versus priorities. It may be the passion for getting the job done that makes it difficult to delegate responsibility. Or, for some, it may be a passion for hobbies that have gotten out of control, such as recreational sports or the Internet. These aren't necessarily vices, but any of them can push our true priorities out of the way.

As I mentioned before, one of the trade-offs I felt forced to make was to give up golf in favor of family time. I enjoyed golf, and early in my career I would play occasionally. But after I was married, I realized that I was giving up large chunks of time to the golf course. That might have been okay, except that I was already giving up *massive* chunks of time to my job. So I had to take inventory: If my family was a priority, as I claimed, how could I justify using such large amounts of my free time each weekend to play golf? My passion was slowly squeezing time away from one of my priorities—my family. For Urban, trying to find the proper balance will be complicated because his life is so public. Most people can work through these decisions privately with the help of a spouse or a trusted friend. Urban has to do it with the entire Gator Nation weighing in. He believes in his heart that he needs to delegate more to be able to spend more time with his family and to protect his health. Everyone agrees that's the right thing to do—unless the Gators don't win the national championship. Then fans will say that he should have spent more time at the office.

I know what he's going through. During my second season in Indianapolis, my family headed home to Tampa over the winter holidays. The Colts were preparing to play the Patriots in the AFC

Championship Game in January 2004, and Nathan, my coauthor, called me one evening about eight o'clock to wish me well that weekend.

He was startled that I answered; he thought he would have to leave me a message. "I just walked into the house," I told him. He asked if my family was gone, and I replied that they were, "But if I had stayed late at the office on a Thursday, then the other coaches—whose families *aren't* out of town—would have felt compelled to stay late, even if I told them otherwise." So even though my family was gone and I could have stayed late, I chose to go home so my coaches would feel better about going home to be with their families. Besides, I've always believed that it takes a certain amount of time to prepare for a game, and once we're prepared, extra time won't help—only execution will.

As it happened, we lost that game 24–14. But staying later wouldn't have changed that. The Patriots simply played better. That night, they were the better team.

In 2007, during the regular season, we played the Patriots in what was billed as "the Game of the Century." (Not the first such game, of course, and certainly not the last.) It was the first time in NFL history that two teams had met that were both undefeated after at least seven games. The Patriots were 8–0, and we were 7–0, having already had our bye week.

> ✛ It takes a certain amount of time to prepare for a game, and once we're prepared, extra time won't help–only execution will.

I had previously agreed to record a public service announcement for The Villages, a home for foster children in the Indianapolis area. We had scheduled it for that week, of all weeks, and I was coming up with a host of reasons why I couldn't do it. After all, the Colts were my employer, not The Villages, and I had players and coaches relying on me. This truly was a big game—the winner would certainly be the favorite to win the AFC Championship and make it to the Super Bowl. But I'd always told those around me, those same players and coaches, that we needed to find balance in our lives with our priorities. If you start making excuses to cut out the things that are important because of urgent circumstances, it will become a habit, and you'll start cutting them out regularly. You know as well as I do that, whether it's a crisis or not, there always seems to be a reason why *this* time just isn't the *right* time.

So, I left a little early on Thursday night and took thirty minutes to record the PSA for The Villages. I felt it was the right decision. On Sunday, we lost 24–20 on a late touchdown by New England, who went on to complete an undefeated regular season and earn a spot in the Super Bowl. We finished the season 13–3 before losing to San Diego in the playoffs. Many people in my position could look back and second-guess that decision to take a half hour away from preparation for the Patriots to help a children's home. If I had watched one more video or gone over one more chart, would we have come up with those four points we needed to win? Would we have ended up in Super Bowl XLII instead of New England? I never lost any sleep over that question, and I will always feel that I gave my best for my team that week.

> ✢ If you start making excuses to cut out the things that are important because of urgent circumstances, it will become a habit.

Please hear what I'm saying: Your employer deserves your loyalty and whatever time it takes to perform your job. However, that job, that career, has to fit into your life in the appropriate place. It cannot *be* your life. It cannot be what defines you. It simply has to be one of the important priorities in your life. There may always be something else you can do to secure a client or land a sale, but you've got to learn to prepare to whatever level is appropriate and then walk away.

Burnout is a common term these days. It is certainly a very real problem, as we never seem to be able to escape the daily demands. E-mail, mobile phones, text messages—all these technological advances are terrific, but they also can leave us without any down-time, or without any time for others who are important to us.

Our employers, whether they realize it or not, need for us to engage in our other priorities because these are the things that recharge and strengthen us. Our relationships and other commitments should leave us more fulfilled and energetic for our jobs and other important pursuits, but they take time and attention for proper care and nurture.

Burnout is a concern in many of our churches, as well. Often when I visit a church, I'll notice the friendly face of the usher holding the door. After the service, when we head off to a Sunday school class, that same usher will be teaching the class. And no doubt this individual is volunteering on Wednesday nights as well.

I think it's fantastic that people are willing to step forward. And I can understand how a church ends up with the same group of volunteers for everything, because certain people just seem inclined to step up. But unless these people also have a chance to be ministered to and to worship in God's presence, instead of always teaching or volunteering, they will burn out. We all need time to recharge our batteries.

+ Our relationships and other commitments should leave us more fulfilled and energetic for our jobs and other important pursuits.

In all these settings—with our families, careers, churches, friends, hobbies, and community involvement—there's no reason to assume that the people most affected by our choices or how we prioritize our time want anything but the best for us. But as we try to figure out how to find a healthy balance in our lives, we need to understand that we all have our own agendas.

So, your employer may truly want the best for you in terms of health and family, and balance between your career and other priorities; but in the end, it may well be that sales figures will be your company's measure of success, and how you perform according to that yardstick may determine the future of your career. In the end, you just need to understand that someone else's agenda cannot determine how you will achieve balance and order the priorities in your own life.

It is ultimately up to each of us to determine the proper balance between our priorities and our passions, based on our understanding of God's direction in our lives, our motivations, and all the other factors that define our individual situations. As we assign priorities to all the important elements in our lives, we will begin to demonstrate our *true* priorities and what is really important to us by what we choose to do first, second, third, and so on. We may *say* that something is important to us, but in the end our actions will determine what we mean. And the people we are trying to influence and guide—our family, friends, team members, employees, and others—will measure our influence by the consistency of our actions and words.

✛ Someone else's agenda cannot determine how you will achieve balance and order the priorities in your own life.

What story will your actions tell?

KNOWING YOUR STRENGTHS

Don't tell me what a player can't do. Show me what he can do and we'll utilize his strengths.

BILL WALSH

Not everything has to be a strength. Limitations are okay, too. We all have them.

Marcus Buckingham, in his book *Now, Discover Your Strengths*, speaks of the importance of knowing our strengths. Too much attention is paid to our weaknesses, he contends, so that we often don't take full advantage of the things we are naturally good at or pursue the things we are naturally inclined toward. He says that instead of spending so much time working on our weaknesses, or on those things we aren't naturally gifted to do, we should surround ourselves with people whose strengths complement our weaknesses.

Chuck Noll took this approach. He didn't try to be all things to all people. He didn't try to change who he was or alter his approach. Instead, he hired coaches with different personalities. I must admit that I didn't notice this when I was playing for him in Pittsburgh, but it became apparent once I was on the Steelers' staff for a while. He always looked for good football coaches who were also good people and who had different strengths that they brought to the team. For instance, he was more of a teacher than a motivator, so having coaches on the staff who were more emotional was important. He taught a certain way, but he hired other guys who taught differently.

I took that lesson with me. In Indianapolis, for instance, I had a lot in common with my quarterbacks coach, Jim Caldwell, who is quiet and introspective; therefore, I thought it was important to have a coach on the staff like Tom Moore, our offensive coordinator, who is very direct and more confrontational than I am. Tom also brought a singleness of purpose to our offensive approach—a tunnel vision that caused us to stick to our system through thick and thin. Mostly thick. And then there was John Teerlinck, the defensive line coach, who brings a fiery passion to his work and sees the world through a much different lens than I do—but an equally good one.

> + We should surround ourselves with people whose strengths complement our weaknesses.

I looked at my age as a factor and a strength, yet also something to complement by hiring coaches of different ages. I was forty when I took the Bucs job and forty-six when I had to make my first major staff overhaul and hire four new coaches. I hired Jim Caldwell, who was my age, as our quarterbacks coach, but on defense I hired Mike Tomlin, Joe Barry, and Alan Williams, who were all in their late twenties. I felt that these three men would be exceptional coaches, but I also felt that because of their ages they would have an easier time relating to some of our players than I would. Youthful enthusiasm was the strength they would bring to our staff, which would offset any weakness they might have in experience. My primary strengths, I always thought, were organizational aptitude and the ability to see the big picture and to continually cast a vision for what we were trying to accomplish and where we were heading. I'm not overly confrontational, and I'm not much for giving motivational speeches. In Tampa Bay, therefore, an important initial hire for me was Herm Edwards, an emotional, high-energy guy.

Where I might analyze facts, Herm was better at reading the energy and emotion of a situation. His strengths helped offset some things I'm not as good at in leading a team.

This principle applies to players, as well. One of the interesting things about coaching the Colts was the wide variety of backgrounds our players had. They came to us from different ethnic and socio-economic groups, and with differing religious beliefs and life experiences. And yet, as the guys got to know each other and worked together, the bonds of commonality grew as the walls between our differences were dissolved.

For example, Reggie Wayne and Peyton Manning both grew up in New Orleans, yet never got to know each other as kids. Reggie went to a predominantly African American public school, and Peyton attended a predominantly white private school. In 2001, they became teammates with the Colts. Their individual strengths and gifts—Reggie as a receiver and Peyton as a quarterback—brought them together on the team with the same common goal. As a result, they came to work closely together and were able to develop a great friendship. And more important, they were able to lead others side by side toward a common goal.

Denny Green, my boss with the Minnesota Vikings, used to say he would not select the fifty-three best *players*, but the fifty-three players who gave us the best *team*. There's a difference between those two approaches, and I learned from Denny that the primary focus should be on choosing the *right* players, just as Herb Brooks said he did with the 1980 U.S. Olympic hockey team. We've all seen examples of "dream teams" that looked great on paper but played like a nightmare, but Coach Brooks took a group of largely unheralded individuals, who were the right combination of players, and put them together to create an exceptionally high-performing team.

With both the Bucs and the Colts, we were fortunate not only to have some of the best players available, with tremendous strengths and skill sets, but also the right players who together made us exceptional as teams through the years.

That, too, was the case with our 2008 U.S. Olympic basketball team. Jerry Colangelo and Mike Krzyzewski worked hard to select a collection of players who would function well as a unit. Although they were criticized after making their selections by people who complained that more talented players had been left off the squad, they were ultimately proved right on the court as the United States won the gold medal, for the first time since 2000.

Part of knowing our strengths and understanding our weaknesses is making a commitment to growth. People respect a leader who doesn't have all the answers as long as they can see that the leader is committed to personal growth. When I was coaching, I was always talking with other coaches, listening to our players, or studying what others were doing to see if there were improvements to be made. Now that I am no longer coaching, I am being mentored in an entirely different arena: broadcasting. I have enjoyed it thus far, and I think I'm improving. But as with coaching, I recognize that there is always room for growth.

✛ **Part of knowing our strengths and understanding our weaknesses is making a commitment to growth.**

You can always improve on both strengths and weaknesses. What it takes is a commitment to growth.

Complementing our strengths with the strengths of others is a recipe for achieving great things together. I find it more useful—and I believe more theologically accurate—to recognize that God has created each of us with different abilities and strengths than to claim that He has limited our potential by instilling weaknesses in us. However, we have to recognize that He has given others incredible strengths and abilities as well, and it's when we are able to humbly combine our strengths with the abilities of others that we really begin to have the makings of something spectacular, something for good.

His good.

ACTION STEPS

1. Take a look inside: Mentor leaders know who they are, what motivates them, and why they do what they do and react the way they react; and they are always ready to change in order to become all that God intends.

2. Evaluate your motives: Are you working for yourself? for God? for others?

3. Come to grips with your past: Get help if you need to. Effective leaders get past the past—the things that tie them down. They realize that forgiveness leads to freedom.

4. Be who you are. Mentor leaders lead as the people God made them to be, and they don't try to be someone else.

5. Evaluate your priorities: Consider the order of importance you place on your relationship with God, your family, your work, your friends, and everything else. Be willing to reevaluate over time.

6. Take a look in the mirror: Recognize that God has given you incredible gifts, abilities, and strengths that are unique to you.

7. Complement your strengths with the strengths of others: Remember, not only were you created for community, but others were too. You were not created to do everything by yourself.

CHAPTER 4

THE MARKS OF A MENTOR LEADER: CHARACTERISTICS THAT MATTER

Wherever you go, I will go.
RUTH 1:16

Leadership experts such as Ken Blanchard, John Maxwell, Jim Collins, the Gallup Organization, the Leadership Research Institute, and countless others have done extensive work to identify core leadership competencies and to improve the skills, strategies, and mechanics of leadership. My goal here is not to supplant their worthy research, but rather to give you my own perspective on the facets of leadership I have found particularly useful for myself and for others whose leadership I have emulated.

I have divided these characteristics into three groupings, which I call *trustworthy traits, leadership attributes,* and *relational qualities.* Please understand that these are simply *my* thoughts on leadership, which spring from an emphasis on mentoring and a desire to add value to the lives of those I lead.

Some of these core competencies are easier to acquire than others, and some may necessitate more development and attention to maintain. Though certain ones may oblige us to rethink our prior assumptions about what it means to be a leader, all of these should be simple enough to understand.

Which personal attributes do you already bring to the table, and which ones do you need to improve? Some traits, such as personality, are what they are, and that's fine. Mentor leaders should simply be who they are. There's no need to try to be someone else.

However, other traits, attributes, and qualities that are central to mentor leadership can be identified, acquired, and improved.

Before we begin that analysis, however, let's look at one competency that stands alone: *character*.

CHARACTER

But the truth is that right actions done for the wrong reason do not help to build the internal quality or character called a "virtue," and it is this quality or character that really matters.
C. S. LEWIS

As critically important as I believe a shared vision is for leadership in an organization, character is even more fundamental and essential. If people aren't comfortable with their leaders—who they are and what they stand for—they won't stick around long enough to hear about the vision. Vision matters, but character matters more.

General Matthew Ridgway, the great American general who led the United Nations forces in the Korean War, stated that character is the foundation on which all leadership is built. He rated character as one of three core leadership skills, along with courage and competence.

Character affects how we interact with the people around us. It influences the kind of people we choose to surround ourselves with. George Washington is reported to have said, "Associate yourself with men of good quality if you esteem your own reputation; for 'tis better to be alone than in bad company."

The apostle Paul, in his second letter to the church in Corinth, reminded the believers that "bad company corrupts good character" (1 Corinthians 15:33). In every setting, we know that the associations we keep tend to paint a picture of our character. And eventually those associations will begin to affect our character.

Although my parents certainly taught me the importance of character, and my mother always told me to choose my friends based on their character, not on whether they were cool or because of what their parents did for a living, I don't think the lessons really settled in my heart until I went to the University of Minnesota to play football for Coach Cal Stoll.

> ✛ **Character is the foundation on which all leadership is built.**

I had looked forward to playing for Coach Stoll when he recruited me, but it wasn't until I arrived on campus that I realized how different he was from my previous coaches. I had no idea how influential he would become in my life, not only during my college career, but for years afterward.

Coach Stoll was the first person I can recall who made the connection between the quality of our character and our success on the football field. He was talking about success in life as well, but what was new to me was the emphasis on character and success in the short-term, on the field. Once I learned that lesson, making the connection to success in life was easy. My high school coach, Dave Driscoll, may have tried to teach us the same thing, but I was probably too young to fully understand what he was trying to get across. Coach Stoll's lessons were the first that really resonated with me.

Much of what we hear today about football players and good character has more to do with their not embarrassing themselves or their school or team than it does with anything else. It's almost as if you have to be a choirboy to have good character. But after playing for Coach Stoll, I've found it is much more than that.

Coach Stoll made the point that *how* we did things affected our results. He further believed that the kind of people we had on our team would affect our ability to get the results we wanted, and that the people we were around would have an impact on us. To follow his thinking, then, the kind of people we spent time with affected our character, and our character affected our performance on the field.

> ✢ The kind of people we had on our team would affect our ability to get the results we wanted.

I had never looked at it that way before. I never thought that my personal life, or that of my teammates, would have any impact on whether we won or lost games. In my mind, winning games was simply a matter of talent and teamwork. So whenever I played pickup basketball on the playground, where the rule was win or sit out—and of course I wanted to win and keep playing—I didn't give any thought to character, just to who could help me win. Or so I thought.

After hearing Coach Stoll, however, I began to think about the decisions I had made over the years and the type of guys I always picked. It hit me that I hadn't necessarily picked the most talented players to be on my team. Some of those guys never passed or didn't play defense. Rather, the guys I picked were the ones who had a burning desire to win and who would do the kinds of things—such as rebounding, defending, or passing to the open man—that would put their team in a position to win. If it meant they didn't score at all in the game, fine. If it meant they scored every point, that was fine too. I realized that, without even thinking about it, I gravitated toward the guys who had character. I began to see that the people I wanted to associate with were people of character both on and off the court or field.

Coach Stoll made it clear that the guys who went to class, who treated other people with respect, and who were responsible in the little things on and off the field were ultimately the ones who gave us a better chance to win. That quality of being responsible in the little things is a key part of a winning attitude.

Ultimately, Coach Stoll showed us that players who weren't reliable off the field would eventually demonstrate those same shortcomings in the heat of battle. If they weren't responsible in other settings, we wouldn't be able to count on them at crunch time. And he was right. That turned out to be true of several of our most talented players at the University of Minnesota, and I saw it play out time and time again over my coaching career.

Surprisingly for some, research conducted by the Leadership Research Institute has shown that in times of crisis, people gravitate toward the person of highest character, not necessarily the person who is "in charge" or even the person they believe to be the most competent. Rather, people will tend to build a relationship with and follow the person they view as the most trustworthy, who cares the most, and who is willing to always do the right thing.

> **+ In times of crisis, people gravitate toward the person of highest character.**

In a crisis, people crave character. But there's no reason to wait for a crisis. You can continue to cultivate your character along the way, and it will contribute to your team's performance long before a crisis ever comes. Character is the glue that bonds solid and meaningful relationships.

TRUSTWORTHY TRAITS

To be trusted is a greater compliment than to be loved.
GEORGE MACDONALD

How we relate as mentor leaders to the people around us will determine whether our organizations will achieve sustained success in pursuing their vision and mission. The qualities we will discuss in the remainder of this chapter are what will set the mentor leader apart from others in this pursuit. Let's begin by looking at the traits that make us trustworthy.

Trustworthy traits are internal qualities that form the bedrock of our character. Regardless of the situation or circumstances, these traits are simply a part of who we are. For the sake of simplicity, I have identified four primary trustworthy traits: *competence*, *integrity*, *security*, and *authenticity*.

Mentor leaders are competent.

To succeed in any endeavor, we have to know what we're doing and why we're doing it. That doesn't mean we have to have all the answers, but it does mean we must have a solid foundation of skill, ability, and knowledge.

The people under our leadership will only continue to follow us if they are satisfied that we are qualified to lead. It's not that they believe we'll never make a poor decision, but that they trust us to guide them well.

✛ As leaders, we must be able to explain why one path is better than another.

As leaders, we must be able to explain why one path is better than another, why our marketing strategy and sales approach is appropriate for the products we're trying to sell, why our practice regimen is this way and not that, or why we expect this play to work against the other team's defense.

Again, we don't need to have all the answers, but the people we lead must be confident that we have the competence to lead them in pursuit of the organization's vision and mission.

Mentor leaders remain focused on integrity.

Integrity is one of the essential building blocks—if not the cornerstone—of any leader's success, but especially that of mentor leaders, who desire to add value to the lives of those they lead. Leadership skills must be built on a proper foundation.

Chick-fil-A, the quick-service restaurant chain founded by Truett Cathy, believes that integrity is so essential to success that they don't attempt to train people for it; they look for it in the people they interview. They believe that if a person doesn't already have integrity, he or she won't achieve it—at least not on Chick-fil-A's dime.

I completely agree.

If the people in your organization can't rely on you—whether on the big things or the little things—how are they going to follow you? They may follow you for a while, but it won't be with passion or full commitment. The reason is simple: When faced with uncertainty about a decision or direction, they won't know whether the person making that decision or pointing them in that direction can be trusted. They may follow for a time, but only conditionally, haltingly, or with misgivings marking every step.

I understand the need for contracts—to trust but verify. But as often as possible, I do business with people I trust, people whose word is sufficient. But whether I trust the other person or not, I make sure that I act in a way that allows him or her to trust *me* completely.

+ **If the people in your organization can't rely on you, how are they going to follow you?**

Integrity is so basic that I won't belabor the point further.

If you have integrity, model it. If you have a problem with integrity, take care of it quickly before your reputation is established as one who is not to be trusted.

Mentor leaders are secure in their own skin.

I know a gentleman who was named CEO of a publicly traded company. As he began to wrap his mind around the challenges facing his company, he called a meeting of his chief lieutenants. Twenty-two people showed up.

At first he thought he had made a mistake. How could so many people possibly report directly to the CEO? As he soon discovered, the previous CEO had been reluctant to delegate authority because doing so would have required him to share information to which only he had access. By ensuring that he was always the only one with all the relevant pieces of the puzzle in a given situation, he protected his own position, but he also failed to train the next generation of leaders.

In contrast, mentor leaders need to exhibit confidence. Not a false bravado, but an inner sense of security—the kind of confidence that doesn't need to be surrounded by yes-men or people trying to curry favor.

From my perspective, a genuine sense of self-worth—the kind of confidence that can't be shaken by circumstances—is best obtained through a relationship with God. The knowledge that He created me and cares for me does more for my mental health and overall well-being than any self-help book ever could. I am both humbled and empowered by the knowledge that Jesus Christ performed the ultimate act of sacrificial service for me. To know that God loves me that much is powerful.

✦ **Mentor leaders need to exhibit confidence. Not a false bravado, but an inner sense of security.**

From that foundation of security comes the ability to mentor others, to lead them without requiring constant affirmation or being crippled by self-doubt. Mentor leadership will never grow from a place of insecurity, like that of the former CEO who attempted to ensure his job security by not sharing pertinent information with others. Mentor leaders are secure enough in who they are that they are able to invest themselves in helping others grow and develop to their full potentials. Secure leaders are free to lift others up who will eventually replace them. It is frustrating to be kept in the dark because of another person's insecurity.

Denny Green, the head coach of the Minnesota Vikings when I was the team's defensive coordinator, was always very good about including me in all aspects of the coaching process. By freely sharing information to help me grow, Denny actively prepared me for the day when I would become an NFL head coach. He exposed me to new situations and decisions on a regular basis, trying to give me a chance to think through issues that would confront me if I became a head coach. He allowed me to interact with the media to build relationships and to practice my skills.

Ironically, as Denny's popularity in Minnesota began to wane over the years, mine began to grow. It's the same syndrome that afflicts starting quarterbacks when the fans clamor for the backup to play—the unknown often seems more appealing than the known. And yet you can always find the true mentor-leader quarterback—on the sidelines, on the practice field, or in offensive meetings—tutoring the backup, helping him grow and become the best he can be. And he does all that with the knowledge that the backup may one day replace him in the starting lineup.

In Minnesota, the situation finally came to a head when a reporter asked me if I would be willing to replace Denny as the head coach of the Vikings were I offered the job.

"Absolutely not," I said. "The Vikings already have a head coach—Denny Green."

"But not if he's fired," the reporter persisted.

"Still no," I said. "I wouldn't be here if it weren't for Denny."

Denny's investment in me—his willingness to elevate my status and prepare me to live out what he believed to be my potential—only served to instill in me more loyalty toward Denny. Sure, his willingness to promote me ended up strengthening his own position because of my resulting loyalty, but that's not why he built into my life. His focus was on trying to help me become the best I could be.

Mentor leaders must be authentic.

To be approachable and secure, to be trustworthy and loyal, you can't be a phony. Above all, mentor leaders must be genuine. People know a fake when they see one.

I am naturally quiet, but as I get to know people better, I begin to open up more and will joke around. Still, I look more serious in public than I do in private. That's who I am, and to be anything else in order to achieve something would be insincere and phony. Someone else can perhaps engage people more easily or be the life of the party. But I don't need to be someone I'm not, nor should I expect others to be something different from who they are. We can all be effective with our own styles. Whatever gifts God has given us, we should make use of them.

> ✦ Above all, mentor leaders must be genuine. People know a fake when they see one.

Be real.

Be authentic.

Be sincere.

People will know when you're not.

And they will know when you are—and be drawn to that.

LEADERSHIP ATTRIBUTES

The "as if" principle works. Act "as if" you were not afraid and you will become courageous, "as if" you could and you'll find you can. Act "as if" you like a person and you'll find a friendship.

NORMAN VINCENT PEALE

Leadership attributes that I believe are intrinsic to mentor leadership include demonstrating courage; leading by example; keeping others focused on the organization's vision and mission; exercising and modeling faith; and always being willing to examine and change paradigms.

Mentor leaders demonstrate courage and are willing to lead by example.

In order to lead effectively, mentor leaders must be willing to get into the trenches. They must get involved. It's not possible to mentor from an ivory tower.

Courageous leadership often means holding firm to decisions we deem to be in the best interests of the organization—even when others disagree.

In 2009, with two regular season games left to play, the Colts were 14–0 and the fans and media were clamoring for them to pursue an undefeated season. But going undefeated was not one of the goals the Colts had set for the season. Accordingly, they took the steps they felt were necessary to achieve their ultimate goal of winning the Super Bowl, which included resting their starters for significant portions of their final two games to keep them healthy. When they lost both games, the coaches were roundly criticized. People debated whether being undefeated *should* have been a team goal, but to me, the decision to rest Peyton Manning and other starters showed a clarity of convictions and the courage to follow them.

+ In order to lead effectively, mentor leaders must be willing to get into the trenches. They must get involved.

Was that the right goal? It doesn't matter. What matters is that *they* believed it was the right goal, and that they took the steps they believed necessary to achieve it, regardless of what people outside the organization said.

It would have been easy for Jim Caldwell, Bill Polian, and Jim Irsay to play the starters for both games and try for an undefeated season. The critical voices quieted—somewhat—when the Patriots'

Wes Welker was injured in week 17 and lost for the playoffs, reminding everyone that injuries can occur to anyone at any time—just what the Colts were looking to avoid. Ultimately, however, whether others believe you are right is not what matters. Instead, it's whether, after listening to counsel and weighing your decision, you have the courage to do what you think is right, regardless of the opposition.

I suppose it's no coincidence that several of my favorite movies include climactic battle scenes and examples of courageous leadership under fire. In *Braveheart*, for example, William Wallace knows he has no chance of victory in an impending battle with the English army. Furthermore, he knows the British will be especially tough on him if he's captured—yet there he stands, at the front of the Scottish lines, exhorting his comrades in the midst of the worst and most difficult circumstances.

The same is true of Aragorn in J. R. R. Tolkien's *The Lord of the Rings* as he rallies his troops against the massed forces of darkness, which far outnumber his men. "A day may come when the courage of men fails. . . . But it is not this day! This day we will fight! By all that you hold dear on this good Earth, I bid you stand, Men of the West!" Often mentor leadership means standing side by side with the people we are leading as they face their greatest challenges.

We are drawn to leaders who are right there in the trenches with us and who are willing not only to stand with us, but also to stand against others on our behalf—leaders who are not above the fray, watching from a distance.

Another great example of a leader who was willing to step down from a place of power and privilege and stand alongside his followers is Jesus Christ. That is partly why Christ's example resonates with us. It would be one thing if He had remained only as God when He came to earth—He still would have provided an example for us and would have deserved our loyalty. But by becoming fully human, He walked among us and experienced much of what we go through. In that, He not only connected with us on our level, but He also gave us a divine role model for leadership, team building, and living our lives with others. He went through what we experience: joys and disappointments, heartache, pain, doubt, and strife.

Leading by example is a powerful way for mentor leaders to forge strong bonds with the people who follow them. But what kind of example are you setting? Do you take shortcuts that others aren't allowed to take? Do you have the courage to make—and stand by—decisions that will be criticized? Do you have the courage to make decisions that are in the best interests of those you lead, regardless of what others may think, even if they temporarily stall the short-term progress of the team?

Mentor leaders keep the vision and mission out front.

When Joe Greene cleaned out his locker and briefly left the Steelers in 1972, he illustrated one of the great challenges facing a mentor leader: keeping everyone on the team focused on and committed to the vision and mission. It's easy to lose sight of the ultimate goal when you are in the trenches—for both the mentor leader and those who are following.

Sometimes occasional reminders are enough. When I was coaching, I met with the team as a whole before and after games and every Wednesday. I took those opportunities from time to time to remind our players of the big picture.

> ✤ **It's easy to lose sight of the ultimate goal when you are in the trenches.**

We also helped them to maintain their focus and commitment by establishing smaller goals within the larger mission for the team. For instance, we divided the sixteen-game season into four quarters and set goals for each quarter. After a hard-fought loss, I reminded the players that our goal for the quarter was to go 3–1. Despite that loss, we were still on track toward our ultimate goal, our ultimate vision and mission—we just needed to focus on what was right in front of us.

During stretches when the team was playing well, I sometimes grew concerned that the players were falling in love with their own press clippings. In those instances, I used the Wednesday meeting to tell a story about pride coming before a fall, to remind them of what we were trying to accomplish, to challenge them to play up to their abilities every week, and to warn them not to become complacent because of the accolades they were receiving.

I was not—and am not—a big believer in continual, unnecessary staff meetings. Our coaches and players had jobs to do, and once they were educated and equipped to do those jobs, I trusted them to function without constant supervision. We met when necessary, and I believed it was my responsibility at those times not to deal with minutiae, but rather to keep them focused on the vision, on who we were as a team and where we were headed together.

Mentor leaders exercise faith.

Faith, simply stated, is belief put into action. It's one thing to state a goal and to create a plan for achieving that goal, but do you really *believe* that your team's effort, when exerted through that plan, will lead to the desired result? As an example of this, Nathan told me about a meeting he had with an NFL general manager, during which they discussed the best way to build a team. Should you do it primarily through the college draft or through free agency? Should you stay well within the salary cap and try to plan for consistency year after year, or does it make sense in a given year to spend beyond the cap (called "cash over cap"), which creates a shortage in future years, in order to take advantage of a "window of opportunity" to obtain an impact player or players? In other words, should you try to win now and worry about the future later, or should you build more gradually and try to establish consistent, long-term success? They also discussed the

+ **Faith, simply stated, is belief put into action.**

role that coaching, off-season training, and a wide range of other topics play in a team's success.

Finally, the GM concluded with this comment: "Look, at the end of the day, winning in this league is as arbitrary as a coin flip."

As Nathan furrowed his brow, the GM continued, "We can plan all we want, and the coaches can coach all they want, but at the end of the day, it's going to come down to whether a fumble bounced our way, or whether our offensive line stayed healthy, or other things that I just can't control."

I agree that there are things beyond our control that can affect the outcome of everything in life. What I don't agree with is his conclusion—that despite the long, tiring hours of preparation and the planning for things that he *could* control, it all came down to a game of chance.

"If it all comes down to chance," he concluded, "then I'd better make sure that nobody can say I was outworked. Even if my effort doesn't matter, at least I can control that, and I can also point back to it when answering my owner, the media, or fans: 'We may have been 5–11, but nobody came in earlier or left later than we did.'"

Faith in the vision and mission is important. Faith in the process and preparation to achieve the mission is important. It makes a difference. You may get a bad bounce, or the coin flip in overtime may not go your way, but the process is important.

Because life is more than a flip of the coin.

As for me, I completely believe that three days is all that is needed to prepare for a football game. *Any* football game. That's a lesson I learned from Chuck Noll and Denny Green. I also believe that time spent beyond those three days is more likely to be unproductive rather than helpful. I was always willing to listen and learn, but I never heard anything compelling that convinced me otherwise. Maybe my approach was wrong, but we posted some pretty solid results over my thirteen years as a head coach using that process, and Chuck Noll and Denny Green had their share of success as well.

Therefore, whether it was the opening game of the regular season, a midseason game against a team with a poor record, or our Super Bowl appearance against the Bears, I approached each game the same way. As a result, I believe our players performed at as high a level as possible over as long a period as possible, achieving consistent, sustainable results. When you are leading, your goal should be to achieve success and significance over the long term, not to be just a flash in the pan.

> ✦ **Long-term success requires faith—faith that your efforts to plan and execute the process will lead to the desired outcome.**

Long-term success requires faith—faith that your efforts to plan and execute the process will lead to the desired outcome. Your team must see your faith and commitment lest they lose sight of the vision, lose faith in the process, and stop following.

I'm a pretty conservative guy. I believe in maxims like not counting your chickens before they're hatched. But at the same time, I also believe that faith must be forward looking. Consider how the writer of Hebrews describes faith: "Faith is the *confidence* that what we hope for will actually happen; it gives us *assurance* about things we cannot see" (Hebrews 11:1, emphasis added).

Sometimes, as a leader, you simply have to act as if the things you believe in will occur. You have to implement positive steps as if the hoped-for result will in fact become reality—you have to put action behind your words.

The Lion, the Witch and the Wardrobe contains a wonderful image of faith in action. In C. S. Lewis's story, Lucy, the youngest of four children, discovers a winter wonderland in the back of an old, magical wardrobe—a tall cabinet used as a coat closet. After experiencing that world, she returns to the present through the doors of the wardrobe and tells her siblings where she has been and what she has seen. Not surprisingly, they greet her story with a chorus of ridicule. Unmoved, and having generated just enough interest in her siblings that they are willing to act on their curiosity, Lucy takes them into the wardrobe with her, and they push through the rows of coats hanging in there and knock on the back wall, as she did on her first journey. This time, however, rather than snow and tree branches, they encounter the solid wood of the back of the wardrobe. No winter wonderland—or wonderland of any sort—appears as she had promised. Nothing but solid wood. Lucy is ridiculed once again, only this time it's more biting and personal.

"That's enough, Lucy."

You've been there, too, right? I know I have. There are always people along the way who are more than willing to suck the joy from any situation, create clouds of doubt, and make sure they've gone on record to say that it can't be done—or, better yet, the classic line that never dies: "We've never done it that way before."

Leading with faith requires a level of optimism that isn't always easy to maintain. Hoping for a desirable outcome—much less having *confidence* and *assurance* that it will happen—requires some mental strength and fortitude. I tried to demonstrate that level of faith to my players and staff, even when times were bleak.

My first year as head coach at Tampa Bay we opened the season with five consecutive losses. Before the sixth game I stood in front of the players and told them that what we were doing would work and to keep the faith. The principles my staff and I were teaching were not new—we'd seen them work with the Steelers in Pittsburgh. They would pay off, but the players had to keep the faith.

+ **Leading with faith requires a level of optimism that isn't always easy to maintain.**

Our faith and our efforts did pay off in Tampa, and the future turned out as we'd envisioned. We finished that year by winning five of our last seven games and went on to finish at .500 or better for the remainder of my time with the Buccaneers.

Of course, as we all know, life doesn't always turn out the way we envision. In 2008, Rod Marinelli stood in front of his Detroit Lions team at 0–6, then at 0–8, then again at 0–15, telling them that the program would work, that things would turn around. He believed it because he'd seen it happen before; Rod was a part of our staff in Tampa Bay that had turned around the Buccaneers. The Lions bought into what he was telling them and played hard, but they finished the year 0–16. No wins. Sixteen losses. When things didn't improve that season, Rod didn't get the chance to be a part of the turnaround. Instead, the Lions changed head coaches during the off-season.

The lesson, however, is still valid. Faith matters. Sometimes our faith is rewarded by seeing things turn around just as we believe they will. Sometimes the clock runs out before what we're planning can come to fruition. But either way, it's important to keep your team focused on the mission and dedicated to the cause. Like Chuck Noll with Joe Greene, don't let your players walk away before the program has a chance to come together.

Walden Media was founded by Mike Flaherty, Cary Granat, and Phil Anschutz to bring the good and meaningful aspects of life to the movie screen. Mike explained that the element of faith was important in bringing *The Lion, the Witch and the Wardrobe* to the big screen. He pointed out to me that Lucy's response to her siblings, who doubted her, was like my experience with the Buccaneers. Both required great confidence and perseverance. Although confronted with doubters all around, some of whom make it personal, Lucy doesn't waver in her belief about the wardrobe and the winter wonderland of Narnia beyond. Though there is no objective proof that the future will be as she claims, she nonetheless *knows* that it will.

The movie version captures the essence of faith perfectly. When Lucy wakes up that night, after being ridiculed by her siblings, the joy and confidence in her heart expresses itself through her actions. She decides to head back to the wardrobe by herself. Bypassing her slippers and instead putting on her wellies—her rubber boots—she smiles in the dark and heads to the wardrobe. She knows that she'll need her boots for the snow awaiting her in the winter wonderland she remembers.

What a wonderful scene: She puts her boots on . . . and smiles.

That says it all. She's not going to check things out first. She could always come back for the boots, but no, they are already on and ready when she walks through the back wall of the wardrobe again . . . and into the winter wonderland she knew would be there.

As leaders, we must lead with confidence in our shared vision and in the future. If we're not optimistic about what awaits us in the future, no one else will be either.

Mentor leaders are always willing to examine and change paradigms.

Mentor leaders, as we will discuss later, should always be willing to learn, to be mentored themselves. This, in turn, means that they are capable of continual growth.

I found it was always better to be open to new—even radical—ideas that might help the team move forward to accomplish all that we were trying to achieve. Because of that, I remained open to new ways of doing things and new ways of approaching problems. And because other people knew that, they were willing to offer ideas and suggestions.

+ **Mentor leaders are capable of continual growth.**

After the 2007 season, some of our veteran players came to me with a suggestion for cutting down our off-season training. All teams get fourteen days for team workouts during the off-season, but our players theorized that because we were in the playoffs every year, we were already getting two or three weeks more practice time than most teams. They felt they would benefit from more recovery time in the off-season.

This was a wild idea to present to a coach: don't take all the practice time you're allowed. But after I thought about it, I realized the players were right. During our Super Bowl year, we played five weeks longer than teams that didn't make the playoffs. Thus, our players shouldn't need as much off-season practice as those other teams did. That year, perhaps to the players' surprise, I agreed to cut our spring workouts in half. The players really had a wise idea, and because they felt free to bring it to me, it stimulated thoughts and produced a better way of doing things. There were other things, of course, that I ultimately would not change, but many issues I was willing to address—and make some changes.

> ✛ The key is being willing to listen—and act.

The key is being willing to listen—and act.

So put your boots on . . . and smile.

RELATIONAL QUALITIES

Personal relationships are the fertile soil from which all advancement, all success, all achievement in real life grows.

BEN STEIN

If trustworthy traits and leadership attributes are the basic building blocks for leadership, then relational qualities are the connective elements between those traits and attributes and the people with whom we interact. As we begin to embrace and develop these relational qualities in our lives, we also enhance the quality of our individual interactions with others.

Mentor leaders are accountable.

It's probably not an overstatement to say that the fate of the planet hung in the balance on the evening of June 5, 1944, as General Dwight D. Eisenhower readied for the events of the following day—Operation Overlord, the Allied invasion of France now known as D-day.

More than six decades later, and with the successful outcome now a part of our history, I'm sure I still don't fully appreciate the uncertainty that Eisenhower faced during that dark night.

Imprecise intelligence information, the German fortifications, the youth of the all-volunteer landing force, and the vagaries of weather along the English Channel all made for doubts as the time for D-day approached. Those doubts had caused Britain's prime minister, Winston Churchill, to only grudgingly give his initial approval to the plan.

That night, the last before the assault, Eisenhower must have felt those doubts all over again. As a result, he penned a message to General George Marshall, his commanding officer, in the event the assault failed. The note reflected an honest reality of the decision making process: no excuses and no explanations. Merely accountability.

✦ In addition to knowing the importance of the cause, they also knew that they answered to a leader who had their backs.

> Our landings in the Cherbourg–Havre area have failed to gain a satisfactory foothold and I have withdrawn the troops. My decision to attack at this time and place was based upon the best information available. The troops, the air, and the Navy did all that Bravery and devotion to duty could do. If any blame or fault attaches to the attempt it is mine alone.*

Is it any wonder that this note never needed to be sent, because the forces of liberation were determined and relentless in their successful drive to free the French and rid the world of the scourge of the Nazis? In addition to knowing the importance of the cause, they also knew that they answered to a leader who had their backs.

---

*See http://www.eisenhowermemorial.org/stories/Ike-accepts-responsibility.htm.

Being accountable is one of the most important things a leader can do. To me, it's closely aligned with character. It's hard to have true character if you can't be accountable. Too often, however, we've seen the contrary.

"I didn't mean what I said."

"It wasn't my fault."

In the NFL, it's not uncommon to see head coaches firing their lieutenants to save their own jobs. In fact, it's almost a postseason ritual.

How many times have we seen a coach fire his offensive or defensive coordinators—or both!—when a season hasn't turned out as planned? Don't get me wrong. Sometimes the assistant coach's job performance or effort isn't up to par, even after continued feedback. Sometimes it's necessary to clean house. But in many cases, the coordinator merely did what he was hired to do or was instructed to do each week.

Until it didn't work out as planned.

✛ **Nothing is more deflating to morale than to have a poor outcome pinned on someone who doesn't deserve it.**

As a head coach, I have been in both situations. Once, in Tampa, I allowed others to influence my decision to fire our offensive coordinator, even though I knew the coordinator was doing exactly what I wanted, exactly what we had agreed he should be doing. I convinced myself at the time that I was saving other jobs by sacrificing one. I also believed I should give deference to those in authority over me.

But that decision is still my single greatest leadership regret. If I had to do it again, I would stand my ground and do what I truly believed was the right thing. It might have meant I was fired, along with my entire staff, but I later realized that I shouldn't have done something my heart was so set against. Sometimes sacrificing one for seventeen is just dead wrong—if it's done for the wrong reasons.

A year later, the replacement I'd hired wasn't working out. He was a good coach and had actually increased our offensive productivity, but he'd turned out not to be the right fit for our staff and situation. So I made the decision to let him go. Both situations hurt me, but in this case, I, as the leader, felt I was making the right decision, and I was able to clearly explain it to my staff.

Nothing is more deflating to morale than to have a poor outcome pinned on someone who doesn't deserve it. It lacks integrity and it overvalues the outcome at the expense of the people, as well as the process. Most of the time, we are only judged on the outcome, whereas the only thing we can control is the process. Make your process the right one and stay true to it.

In any event, leaders who are accountable earn the respect of those they lead. Without that respect, they cannot lead for long.

Mentor leaders understand the importance of being available and approachable.

It used to be common for leaders to keep their distance from the people they led. When I was growing up, the legendary college football coaches were often pictured coaching from a tower, watching over the entire field from fifty feet above and shouting instructions through a bullhorn. The prevailing wisdom at the time said, "Don't get too close to those you lead." Difficult decisions would have to be made. Layoffs. Restructurings. A different focus. If you got too close, it would be too difficult to "lead" and make the tough decisions "for the good of the order."

> ☩ **The best leaders I've found are those who are engaged with the people around them.**

Because relationships might cloud the leaders' judgment, it was thought that they should stay aloof and above the daily fray.

I think most of us have now gotten beyond that old model. The best leaders I've found, over a lifetime of coaching and speaking with other leaders in sports and business, are those who are engaged with the people around them.

When you know the people who are following you, maybe some of the decisions get tougher. Maybe they are more painful. Maybe the additional information you have—about a person's home life, family, finances, or personality—might make a particular decision more difficult. But you aren't looking for easy, I hope.

Being available and approachable is necessary for effective leadership. Moreover, for me, it's a part of who I am. To try to pull back and away—as if I am not willing to be involved or don't care—or to be viewed as aloof is not only contrary to who I am, but it's not what God wants from me. And I don't believe it's what God wants in the kind of leaders we need in the world today.

✛ **Being available and approachable is necessary for effective leadership.**

It's not what a mentor leader is meant to be.

Being available and approachable isn't always as easy as it might sound, however. Being available—available to teach, available to interact, available to care—also means being involved. But by allowing others to approach you, and by being open to and sincerely welcoming interaction in your leadership role, you'll have the opportunity to relate to people on a much more meaningful basis. It will pay enormous dividends for you and your organization in both the short and long term.

First of all, as your relationships deepen, you will build trust, and your open-door policy will provide an environment in which even more mentoring can occur. Second, as the bonds of friendship grow, the people you lead will grow more committed to you—because it is clear that you care about them. And the goals that seem worthwhile to you will have value to them. They will go out of their way to help you and the rest of the team succeed.

Part of being approachable is staying available emotionally. Jim Zorn, the former head coach of the Washington Redskins and long-time quarterback for the Seattle Seahawks, is part of a weekly Bible study conducted over the telephone with me and a number of other coaches. He said that he picked up a phrase during his career that helped him when the pressure was on: "Act medium." I had to admit that I'd never heard that one before.

Jim explained that in football, as in life, it's easy to be buffeted by the ups and downs of the moment—by our emotions. It's obvious that we can be shaken by negative moments. We've all had negative reactions to bad calls, stresses, and troubles that can cause us to be slow to respond or to make poor decisions. It can happen in good times as well. Jim said that when he was a young quarterback, he tended to dwell on the results of the first half of games. If he played well, he tended to get too high and think, *I've done my job*, and then he would rest on his laurels and not focus as well on the second half. If he played poorly, he would tend to get down on himself and not feel confident that he could play better in the second half.

Over time, he learned to put things behind him emotionally—both good and bad—and to stay focused on future performance. Thus, to "act medium" came to mean staying available emotionally—neither too high nor too low, avoiding either extreme.

Mentor leaders exhibit loyalty to those they lead.

I don't think I could ever overestimate the value of loyalty. It is fundamentally important to mentor leadership.

Loyalty, of course, is related to integrity and trustworthiness, but it's also slightly different. Loyalty involves being faithful to something or someone—a team, a mission, or an individual. Simply being trustworthy does not necessarily demonstrate loyalty. I could keep someone's trust without caring about him or her. Loyalty takes trustworthiness and integrity to another level.

One of the finest examples of loyalty can be found in the Bible, in the book of Ruth. At the beginning of the story, Naomi is left in a foreign land with her two daughters-in-law, Ruth and Orpah; all three of the women are widowed. Naomi tells the two young women to return to their families, and Orpah reluctantly does so. Ruth, however, refuses to leave, saying, "Don't ask me to leave you and turn back. Wherever you go, I will go; wherever you live, I will live. Your people will be my people, and your God will be my God. Wherever you die, I will die, and there I will be buried. May the LORD punish me severely if I allow anything but death to separate us!" (Ruth 1:16-17). That response—that *loyalty*—makes

+ **Loyalty takes trustworthiness and integrity to another level.**

sense when you look at Naomi's leadership and the compassion she showed to Ruth in what must have been challenging times.

Loyalty develops depth in a relationship, which then forges the bonds to hold the relationship firm and fast when storms and challenges come. And they will come. When mentor leaders demonstrate their loyalty time and time again to those they lead—in both their personal and professional lives, those relationships will be fortified to withstand whatever challenges they face. Adversity will come. It's guaranteed. Life is not a matter of smooth sailing. Sometimes the sails are trimmed and the wind is at our backs, but that kind of sailing doesn't last forever in this life. The storms will come, and the waves will crash over even the strongest of relationships, teams, organizations, families, and individuals. That's when proven loyalty will provide the strength and perseverance necessary to help those relationships survive and come out stronger when the storm passes.

Proven loyalty, believed and embraced by the people you serve and lead, will go a long way toward unifying your organization into one that can face every challenge—together.

Mentor leaders shepherd and protect their followers.

I was a young coach in the late 1980s, working for the Pittsburgh Steelers. I had learned a lot over the course of my playing career, and now that I was coaching under Coach Noll, I was always willing to keep learning.

As I continually looked for examples of what it meant to be a good leader, I found a great one in John Thompson, the Hall of Fame basketball coach of the Georgetown University Hoyas. Coach Thompson was a crusader in many respects, having become the first African American coach to lead a team to the Final Four, in 1982, and the first African American coach to win the NCAA Division I national championship, two years later.

Along with his success, he always seemed to find himself in the middle of controversy—probably from a combination of his fiery temperament and his willingness to be a trailblazer for individual rights and fundamental fairness for everyone. He took a stand on everything from the NCAA's reliance on standardized testing to how much access to his players the media should be granted. His protectiveness of his players was seen in a negative light by many in the media, spawning the term "Hoya Paranoia."

But despite his reputation as a rough, gruff coach, one demonstration of Coach Thompson's "paranoia" made a profound impact on my attitude as a coach and what it meant for me to care for my players.

During the 1980s, Rayful Edmond III was one of the most notorious drug dealers in Washington, DC. His network was thought to be responsible for numerous murders, and he reportedly was one of the first dealers to introduce crack cocaine into the District of Columbia. Unfortunately for Coach Thompson, Edmond became a big fan of Georgetown basketball and their great success.

When Coach Thompson learned that Edmond was fraternizing with some of his players, including star center Alonzo Mourning, he sent word to Edmond through them, requesting a meeting on the Georgetown campus. Coach Thompson was well aware of the rumors linking Edmond and his organization with violence and murder, but he quickly got to the point when Edmond arrived:

Edmond was never again to wear Georgetown gear, and he was to have no further contact with any of the Georgetown players. I don't know this for a fact, but the word on the street was that Coach Thompson made his point with words and an attitude that Edmond would clearly understand.

I tried to put myself in John Thompson's shoes. I simply couldn't see myself confronting Edmond directly. I probably would have started by meeting with Mourning, explaining to him the dangers of being around a drug dealer like Edmond, or maybe instituting a team rule limiting where players were allowed to go. Or maybe I would have gone as far as to approach the police, explaining the situation and looking for guidance and help—in other words, get someone who was trained in that environment to handle it. I was pretty sure I wouldn't have stood face-to-face with a reputed killer.

But then it hit me. I immediately thought of Jesus' parable of the sheep and the shepherd in the Gospel of John, chapter 10. There, Jesus speaks of the difference between a hired hand and a shepherd. When a wolf comes and threatens the flock, the hired hand runs away, leaving the sheep—someone else's sheep—to fend for themselves. The shepherd, on the other hand, rises to the defense of his sheep. He will *die* for the sheep, if necessary, because they are *his*.

+ **When a wolf comes and threatens the flock, the shepherd rises to the defense of his sheep.**

I knew that Coach Thompson cared for his players—he had long had that reputation. But by putting himself directly in the middle, between his players and danger, he showed me just how much he loved them.

It wasn't that he knew Alonzo Mourning and the others were talented players who could help Georgetown win games. That wasn't the point. Coach Thompson had told the players and their parents that he would watch over them as if they were his own. He did that, even to the point of placing himself in harm's way.

It was a good lesson for me. I had to take a look in the mirror to determine whether I was exhibiting this relational quality: I cared about those I was leading, but was I willing to die for them if that became necessary for their well-being? I hoped the answer was yes, but I wasn't sure that it was—yet.

Coach Thompson's example made me think about my attitude toward the players I coached. I had always wanted them to be better players as a result of my coaching, and I had always been concerned about them as people. But now I began to see it as more than just a player–coach relationship. I realized that I needed to be more like the shepherd than the hired hand in protecting my team. From there I began to build the family atmosphere that eventually became a hallmark of our teams.

> ✚ Character—the fundamental mark of effective leadership.

Character—the fundamental mark of effective leadership. Keep striving to attain it, as well as the other core traits, attributes, and qualities of a mentor leader.

ACTION STEPS

1. Review the trustworthy traits, leadership attributes, and relational qualities discussed in this chapter and evaluate whether you need to give additional attention to them in your own life.

2. Are you accountable? Think hard about how those around you would describe you to others. Are you the kind of person who would be likely to "throw them under the bus"?

3. Do you accept responsibility when appropriate, or do you always look to place the blame on others?

4. Do you make sure that people are recognized—specifically, by name, where appropriate—when credit is to be given?

5. If you are not presently accountable, look for ways in which others can see that you are willing to share the responsibility for things that go wrong.

6. Do you live with integrity? Take an honest look at whether others would agree that your word is your bond. Can people take you at face value, or would they need something in writing to back up your word?

7. Many people still resist the idea that leaders should be available and approachable. Evaluate your own perspective. Do you push back, hiding behind the attitude that you are too busy to hear directly from those around you? If you have too many direct reports, evaluate your attitudes about delegation, empowerment, and trust. Determine how you can begin to build strength into the people you lead.

8. Are you loyal? When was the last time you went to bat for someone, especially against the tide of popular opinion? As a decision starts to gather momentum, do you shift to the winning side, or are you willing to stick to your guns? When your team is not in the room, do they believe that you will fight for them and their ideas? If not, look for small steps that will allow you to build up others' faith in your loyalty.

9. Are you comfortable with not being the most knowledgeable person in the room? Are you secure enough to teach and share with others the things you know that will help them to be better at what they do?

10. Are you the same person in public as you are in private? Are you authentic? Can people rely on your sincerity?

11. It has been suggested that character is demonstrated when no one is watching. Are you a person of character? Can others trust you when they're not around? Just as important, are you helping and encouraging others to build their character as well?

12. Are you shepherding those around you? your family? the people you lead? Would you place yourself in harm's way

for their sakes—either physically, as Coach Thompson did, or professionally?

13. Are you willing to change? Are you continuing to develop your knowledge and skill to become the most competent person you can be?

14. Do you exhibit faith in what you're asking others to believe in?

CHAPTER 5

THE MOMENTS OF A MENTOR LEADER: INFLUENCE AND IMPACT

The least movement is of importance to all nature. The entire ocean is affected by a pebble.

BLAISE PASCAL

Mentor leaders look for opportunities in life to make an impact, because those opportunities to make a difference in the lives of others will *always* be present. Don't worry about the size of your platform or whether you'll have one—you will. Instead, pay attention to the people around you and the opportunities in front of you, knowing that your chances to make a positive difference will come along in due time. If you pursue mentor leadership, God will ultimately use you for His good; and He is capable of accomplishing more than you ever thought possible. Focus on the impact you can have with the platform God gives you.

You are in a place that no one else occupies. Your family, your friends, and your workplace are all spheres of influence that no one else has in quite the same way; therefore, no one else can make a difference in those areas like you can.

Too often I hear people say that they will make a difference—*later*. Once they've accomplished more, once they have more free time, once the kids are grown and gone. But in the meantime, how many opportunities are lost to change someone's life—a life that may not otherwise be changed? Don't let your age—either young or old—or your experience, or the call of success get in the way of your mission to touch the world for good. You stand where no one else stands. Open your eyes and your heart and look for opportunities.

Mentor leaders are always looking to make a positive difference—whether directly, through mentoring; indirectly, by being a role model; or through unexpected special situations that come along in life. Constant awareness of the opportunities we have to make a difference in other people's lives is what distinguishes mentor leadership from other leadership models I've seen. Every opportunity matters—regardless of size.

> ✛ You stand where no one else stands. Open your eyes and your heart and look for opportunities.

Those opportunities matter to someone; and because of that, they matter to God.

PLATFORMS: CHANGING THE WORLD, ONE LIFE AT A TIME

If you can't feed a hundred people, then feed just one.
MOTHER TERESA

We are surrounded by countless moments in which we can influence others. Ideally, our influence will be for good—but that depends on us. We will choose from day to day, or from situation to situation, what kind of influence we will be. That's the power we have to make a difference in the world around us.

Our impact could be as simple—and as profound—as changing

one life. And in that moment of changing a life, we will begin to leave our legacy.

Understand that we all will leave a legacy. The only question is what kind of legacy we will leave—positive or negative. It's not a question we should put off until our last days on earth. It's something we must think about now, each and every day that we live.

Don't worry about your platform; focus on your impact. One way or another, you *will* have a platform. God will supply it. How you use the opportunities you're given to affect the world around you will determine the legacy you leave behind. It's up to you to use whatever platform you're given to be a positive influence in other people's lives.

Mentor leaders understand that leadership is not about authority, direction, or control, though each, in its proper place and time, is appropriate. Instead, the focus of the mentor leader is on adding value to people's lives.

✛ **Don't worry about your platform; focus on your impact.**

Every platform is important in God's eyes. Make the most of yours.

You've been entrusted with a unique set of circumstances, relationships, and opportunities. No one else stands precisely where you do. Your day-to-day relationships elevate you to a singular position of importance in the lives of your family, friends, coworkers, teammates, and neighbors—the people all around you. They believe in you and derive value from your input. No one else can have the same impact in their lives.

I've heard too many people say that because they aren't professional coaches, or because they are too young or too old, they can't lead. That's unfortunate. Think of the mentors you've had in your own life. Were any of them rock stars? Did they have huge platforms in terms of the number of people they could reach? My mentors didn't—not the truly meaningful ones in my life. If you're like me, your mentors are probably your parents, your teachers, a boss, your friends' parents, or a coach.

As the apostle Paul writes, "Each of us did the work the Lord gave us. I planted the seed in your hearts, and Apollos watered it, but it was God who made it grow. It's not important who does the planting, or who does the watering. What's important is that God makes the seed grow. The one who plants and the one who waters work together with the same purpose. And both will be rewarded for their own hard work" (1 Corinthians 3:5-8). We are all placed in different situations. Sometimes we're there to plant a seed, other times to water or cultivate a seed that someone else has planted. And sometimes we're called upon to help in the actual harvest. From our limited human perspective, we often esteem one opportunity more than another. But God doesn't see it that way. Every platform He sets before us has a purpose in His plan. Every platform creates a unique opportunity to change the world by changing people's lives.

Age—at either end of the spectrum—shouldn't be a limitation or an excuse not to mentor someone. Again, that's our limited human perspective, not God's. Sometimes we don't even realize the effect we have on other people as we go about our business. After Nathan left for college, he learned that a player from another high school in his hometown had traveled to watch Nathan's baseball games whenever possible. This young man, Jeff, was two years younger than Nathan, and Nathan didn't know him. But Jeff's dad had spotted Nathan at a game one time, had liked the way Nathan conducted himself in good times and bad, and wanted Jeff to emulate Nathan's behavior. All that time, Nathan had never realized that anyone was coming to watch *him* play baseball. So, you never know when your example might be used to build into someone else's life.

✛ **Every platform creates a unique opportunity to change the world by changing people's lives.**

It was the same for me. One of my mentors was Allen Truman, a young man who was five years older than I was. Allen was born in Jackson, Michigan, and still lives there today. For some reason, when I was twelve or thirteen, he took me under his wing. I'm still not sure why. Maybe it was because he had lost his father when he was fifteen. Whatever his reason, Allen chose to intentionally invest his time in me. He saw it as a chance to lift someone else up. There may have been other kids that he mentored as well, but it didn't seem like it to me. He had been my coach on a peewee baseball team, but when I became a teenager, he started doing things one-on-one with me—taking me to the gym to shoot baskets, driving me different places to play basketball with older guys. He took me to Detroit to attend Tigers games and Pistons games, and to East Lansing for Michigan State basketball games. It seems as if he took me all over the place, wherever he happened to be going. I can't think of a whole lot of eighteen-year-olds—then or now—who would do that, but I'm grateful that Allen did.

It made a difference in my life.

Sometimes it was just the two of us; other times he would bring other guys along—his brothers or cousins. He would often ask if I just wanted to hang out, and I, of course, always said yes. He didn't have any special "mentor training" or a clear plan or agenda, but what he had was some time and the willingness to invest it in someone like me. He was willing to take a younger neighborhood kid out and about, wherever he was going, and to show him, without even having to say it—although sometimes he did—that you didn't have to run with the crowd.

I'll remember forever Allen telling me I had special gifts. He reinforced what my parents were telling me—that I could do whatever I wanted if I set my mind to it—and he offered advice. Those were moments that lifted me for years to come, having someone tell me I had the potential to do good things in the future. Allen also counseled me about things to avoid. He told me about guys he had seen who had the same potential I did, but who hadn't taken advantage of their opportunities. He was truly a big brother and a mentor to me, someone who did what he could to guide me and to help me successfully navigate the potential pitfalls of my teenage years.

Unfortunately, when I hit eighteen, I wasn't as self-aware as Allen was. That's a nicer way of saying I was too self-centered and insensitive to see that I might have been able to have a similar impact on the life of another young person. I was driven to get better and was hanging out with guys my own age, getting ready for college or off at college, and I didn't give any thought to any thirteen-year-olds in my neighborhood who might have needed a mentor. Frankly, I was only thinking about helping myself at that point. I was looking for older guys to play with so I could get better, not looking for someone younger who might need guidance. There's no reason why I couldn't have done both.

Today, as I reflect on what Allen did for me, I realize there's no excuse for my not recognizing the opportunities I had to be a positive influence in the lives of the younger boys who were all around me—boys I could have lifted, encouraged, and guided.

I'm sure that's one of the reasons I'm always looking to do things with young people now, especially boys. I've learned that I have to be intentional. I need to be intentional about being a mentor, recognizing my platforms and taking advantage of the opportunities I have to impact people around me. It's all too easy to slide along, especially now that, it seems, there are fewer informal times to interact with other people. Our lives are so structured. For so much of our lives we're on call.

It was easier, in some respects, when I was growing up. Jackson, like many communities then, had a fully funded and active recreation program. We had great recreational and sports programs that were staffed by college students who were home for the summer—exactly the people that we younger kids were naturally looking up to anyway.

But when I was in college at Minnesota, I didn't participate in the programs at home. Instead, I stayed on campus, worked well-paying summer jobs in Minneapolis, and honed my athletic skills after work. That's why I'm so proud of the many Colts players I had who went into the Indianapolis high schools to coach and tutor in the off-season. We all need to realize the platforms we have and take advantage of the mentoring opportunities they provide. It's easy to get wrapped up in our own busy lives, but there are opportunities all around us where we can make a difference in someone's life. We just need to look for them.

✛ I need to be intentional about being a mentor, taking advantage of the opportunities I have.

Not everyone will have the same impact.

When we realize that we were all created with different gifts and abilities, it seems obvious that we also have different opportunities and levels of impact. The apostle Paul tells us that the body of Christ is made up of different parts, each one benefiting the body in a different way: "There are different kinds of service, but we serve the same Lord. God works in different ways, but it is the same God who does the work in all of us" (1 Corinthians 12:5-6).

My father taught me this one day when I was complaining about something. I don't remember why I was complaining, but I do remember his primary lesson, as well as another one that I took from it.

After listening to me vent for a while, my father finally told me a story about a time when he was teaching high school science in Alexandria, Virginia. It was his first teaching job, and it was a time when the Alexandria school system was still segregated, in the days of separate-but-equal laws in education.

He said that at first he would sit in the all-black school and wonder if it was true—was it really equal? Just what did the all-white schools look like? And why couldn't these children who were sitting in his classroom go to that school—and why couldn't he teach there?

The easy thing, he made sure to tell me, would have been to slide down that slippery slope into a whirlpool of constant complaining about what a terrible system it was. Sure, the system was wrong and needed to be fixed, he said. But until it was fixed, the real question was, What can *I* do with the platform I have? What solutions can *I* offer? Just complaining did nothing to help the children in his classroom, and it would have distracted him from seeing the opportunity he had before him—to have a positive impact on his students' education and ultimately on their lives.

+ **Stop complaining and act. Do something to make the situation better.**

To my dad, it was crystal clear. The kids in his classroom needed to learn science *right then*. They couldn't wait for the situation to change. His mission at that point was to make sure his students knew as much about science as the students in the other building. And God had equipped him to do something about that.

That's the mind-set of a mentor. It's a mind-set that sees the platform *as it is*—not as it someday may be—and takes action *now*. It's a mind-set that focuses on having a positive impact on others, wherever they may be.

Of course, when my dad told me that story, I focused on his immediate point: Stop complaining and act. Do something to make the situation better. I wasn't thinking about how his example—played out by countless others of his generation in countless other schools, workplaces, and communities—would one day bear fruit.

Years later, in 2007, I had the chance to visit the White House with the Indianapolis Colts after our Super Bowl victory. We landed at Reagan National Airport, just minutes from Alexandria, and as we drove to the White House to meet with President George W. Bush, I couldn't help but think about my dad, who had died three years earlier. What a difference a generation had made. My father had not been allowed to teach at the white high school in Alexandria, and now his son was driving through that city on his way to visit the president. Just two years later, I would return to the White House to witness the inauguration of our first African American president. Yet another example of how far the country had come in a single generation.

Today I realize how my dad helped in that journey. No, he wasn't a vocal trailblazer in the civil rights movement. His name will never appear in the history books, like those of Martin Luther King Jr. or Rosa Parks. But by turning out a great group of tenth-grade science students, my dad used the platform he had at the time to make a big difference in a few young lives.

Wilbur Dungy never made it to the White House, but I know I wouldn't have made it there without him. Your platform may not include an audience with the president, but it is important, and it has the potential to change the world, one life at a time.

UNEXPECTED OPPORTUNITIES

The greatest good you can do for another is not just to share your riches, but to reveal to him his own.

BENJAMIN DISRAELI

Opportunities for influence may arise when least expected. I suppose that's obvious, but it's something we need to keep in mind. A chance meeting. An unexpected introduction. An otherwise normal situation in which our attention is drawn to someone in need. It may be a critical moment in someone's life—a special chance to make a lasting difference. I was on the receiving end of one such special opportunity, and I'm grateful that the man with the platform—Mr. Rockquemore, the assistant principal at my junior high school—was ready, willing, and able to respond.

For most junior high students, the assistant principal was someone you didn't want to run into because he was in charge of discipline and setting the rules and policies for the school. It probably wasn't supposed to be like this, but the principal and his assistants always instilled fear in students. I can remember thinking in eighth grade that if you interacted with Mr. Rockquemore, it was probably not for a good reason. But I was about to learn the difference between perception and reality.

✛ **Opportunities for influence may arise when least expected.**

Mr. Rockquemore was different. On one of the first days of school, he came over and sat down by a group of us boys in the lunchroom. He didn't say anything at first; he just sat there next to us and listened as we continued to talk through our lunch period. Of course, we were on our best behavior, trying to figure out what he wanted from us. We figured that one of us must have done something wrong and he was trying to find out who it was—so of course we didn't bring up anything that might incriminate us.

But our apprehension turned to shock when Mr. Rockquemore started asking us about things outside of school—such as what we thought of the Jackson 5 or what was going on with the Detroit Tigers.

These conversations started happening on a regular basis. He would find us, and others, and simply sit and talk about things we wanted to talk about, things that he felt were of interest to us. He might ask us about another team's best player and how we were going to handle him when we played. Or what was going on with our brothers and sisters. It surprised me how much he knew about things that were going on in our lives away from school. Our initial shock turned to puzzlement, trying to figure out why Mr. Rockquemore was doing this.

Why is he spying on us?

What does he want?

We asked ourselves the same questions you might ask if the boss came and sat with you at lunch—since bosses and assistant principals typically don't do that. It took us a while, but we finally figured out his ulterior motive: He was trying to learn more about us because he cared about us.

Who would have guessed?

Funny thing is, we really began to enjoy having Mr. Rockquemore around, and we developed a trust with him over time. Occasionally he took us to the high school football or basketball games—it turned out he was quite a sports fan. And he kept up with us even after we had graduated from Frost Junior High.

I shouldn't have been surprised, then, when Mr. Rockquemore took it upon himself to mentor me after I quit the high school football team before my senior season. I tell the full story in *Quiet Strength*, but for purposes of our discussion about mentor leadership, here are the essential facts.

When I was selected to be a team captain and one of my closest friends, Bobby Burton, was not, I convinced myself that the decision had been made because they didn't want two black captains. Being something of a hothead at the time, I responded by quitting the team and several other black players followed suit. We skipped winter conditioning and missed the summer workouts. Then, right before fall practice was to begin, Mr. Rockquemore, who was aware of the situation and clearly thought I was making a mistake, invited me over to his house. He reminded me of how much I enjoyed playing football and of the responsibility I had as a leader to the other boys who had quit the team with me, and he challenged me to reconsider my decision. I'll never forget the question he asked me, which ultimately changed my mind: "Why would you let *anything* stop you from doing what you have the ability to do?" I couldn't argue with his logic, and it was clear that he cared enough about me to get involved when he didn't have to. So, I swallowed my pride—which was no easy feat—and returned to the team for my senior year. And here I am now, writing about leadership lessons learned over a thirty-one-year NFL career. I didn't know it at the time, but Mr. Rockquemore was a true mentor leader, and his willingness to get involved changed the course of my life.

I learned two important lessons from what Mr. Rockquemore did, beyond the ones he was teaching me at the time. First, you can't lead in a vacuum; leadership is all about relationships. And second, never underestimate your platform—especially the one right in front of you.

✛ **You can't lead in a vacuum; leadership is all about relationships.**

The relationship that Mr. Rockquemore had built with me in junior high was critical to what happened later. I would never have gone to his house that summer if he were just the junior high school assistant principal. It wasn't his position that gave him influence; it was the relationship he had developed. Because of all the time Mr. Rockquemore had spent with my friends and me during those lunch breaks and other times, and because of what he had built into our lives just by caring, I was more than willing to go speak with him, even though I was seventeen and in high school. The relationship he had established with me provided the opportunity for mentoring, instruction, and a positive influence in my life.

Never underestimate your platform.

Sociologist Tony Campolo tells the story of an elderly man who walked into Tony's tough Philadelphia neighborhood, knocked on his door, and invited him to a Sunday school class. From that simple act, Tony claims that his entire career and ministry were launched.

As for Mr. Rockquemore, all he did was save one young kid from quitting the high school football team. Big deal. From his platform as assistant principal at Frost Junior High School, he saw an opportunity to build into another person's life, to mentor a young man who he felt was about to get off track. No big deal, really—at least not at the time. But that moment flashed through my mind as I was standing on a platform after the Super Bowl in Miami, as the first African American coach to win the Super Bowl, and knowing that my words that night would be heard by hundreds of millions of people.

No big deal? You never know what kind of impact you might have in someone's life. And you may never know what God will do with those moments to achieve His purpose for the benefit of others. You just never know.

Opportunities to make a difference—to have an impact—may come when least expected.

Be ready for them.

And never underestimate the difference you can make in someone's life. It might even be a difference that lasts for eternity.

INDIRECT OPPORTUNITIES: ROLE MODELING

You never get a second chance to make a good first impression.
WILL ROGERS

We are all role models. There is simply no escaping it. Whether we're completely unaware—as Nathan was in high school when young Jeff was watching his every move on the baseball field—or very intentional, as Colts linebacker Gary Brackett is for thousands of kids, we are all role models for someone. There is simply no escaping it.

✛ **We are all role models for someone. There is simply no escaping it.**

What kind of role model are you? Well, that's another matter altogether.

One of my early role models in coaching and leading a team was the Cowboys' Tom Landry. (I probably shouldn't admit that, especially not in print, since I was on the other side of those great Steelers/Cowboys rivalries in the 1970s and '80s.)

My first recollection of Coach Landry, when I was still in high school, was watching his responses to the behavior of running back Duane Thomas. Thomas had been drafted in the first round, with the thought that he might replace Calvin Hill; but instead he was traded to the New England Patriots after his rookie year. The Patriots, however, voided the trade almost immediately, sending Thomas back to Dallas. Thomas then vowed not to speak to any player, coach, or anyone else in the Cowboys organization during the 1971 season.

Coach Landry never flinched in treating Duane with grace and fairness. His goal was to blend Thomas's incredible playing skills with the team's other talented players to create success rather than disruption. Thus, he never made an issue of Duane Thomas's "vow of silence." I'm sure at some point during the year, Duane had to speak to someone in the Cowboys organization, but it was obviously not an ideal situation. Coach Landry was somehow still able to lead that team to a Super Bowl victory.

At some point during his time with the Cowboys, Thomas even referred to Coach Landry as "plastic," which, frankly, seemed to fit my impression of the coach from a distance. You never heard a response from Coach Landry, but I suspect if you had watched him closely when he heard Duane's characterization of him, you might have seen a wry smile.

Coach Landry seemed stoic and placid, emotionally immovable on the sidelines, and incredibly calm in his demeanor. His teams, of course, were very good, but you never saw or heard a lot of that attributed to Coach Landry. The Cowboys were called America's Team, but I never heard anyone refer to Coach Landry as America's Coach. I'm sure that's just the way he wanted it.

A few years later, when I arrived in Pittsburgh, Coach Landry went from being a coaching curiosity to being an archenemy. But it wasn't until I began my own coaching career with the Steelers that I realized just how far ahead of his time Coach Landry was with many of the things the Cowboys did on the field—which were totally different from what the rest of us in the league were doing. In fact, Tom Landry was ahead of his time in a lot of ways, including how he led a team.

I later got to know some of the players who played for Coach Landry—guys like Tony Dorsett—who said that their coach was the genuine article, a man who lived out the Christian principles he quietly espoused. I then started reflecting more on his manner and methods and on how he was successful for so long in a city that placed such high expectations on the Cowboys. More surprising was that Coach Landry was able to keep such a low profile in a town that loved its superstars. But he succeeded in keeping the focus on the players rather than on himself.

Tom Landry ultimately became one of my heroes in coaching—a true role model, who proved it was possible to live your life according to Christian principles and yet still be ultrasuccessful. He showed me that it was possible to lead and coach without compromising.

Two other coaching role models for me were Emlen Tunnell and Art Shell. Tunnell played at the University of Iowa and was the first African American to play for the New York Giants. Art Shell, meanwhile, played at Maryland State–Eastern Shore and then went on to a distinguished career with the Oakland Raiders. Both men are in the Pro Football Hall of Fame as players, but it was their being role models as coaches that really made me take notice of them and had a lasting impact on me as a person and as a coach.

Both Tunnell and Shell were known as cerebral players who studied and really understood the game—which is why they both got an opportunity to coach in the NFL in an era when many blacks weren't getting that opportunity. With their leadership ability and football knowledge, they were able to overcome the prevalent stereotypes of the time and break down barriers for others, like me, who would follow in their footsteps.

In 1957, eleven years after the NFL had integrated the playing ranks, Tunnell became the first African American to coach in the NFL, as a defensive player-coach with the New York Giants. Incidentally, Tom Landry began his coaching career as a player-coach with the Giants three years prior to Tunnell, and he was also a defensive assistant coach in New York when Tunnell began his coaching career. In 1989, Art Shell became the first African American head coach in the modern NFL, thirty-two years after Tunnell had blazed the trail. They were role models, not only because of their status and courage as pioneers, but also because of their intellectual and positive leadership approaches to playing and coaching football.

Regardless of our situations in life, we are always role models for someone—*always*—and probably in ways we wouldn't expect. My son Eric has long looked up to Larry Fitzgerald, the wide receiver for the Arizona Cardinals. That's not surprising because Larry is one of the most gifted players in the league.

> ✦ Regardless of our situations in life, we are always role models for someone—*always*.

But the real reason Eric watched Larry's every move in the NFL was because of where Larry started—as a ball boy for the Minnesota Vikings. You see, Eric also started out as a ball boy for my teams, and he hopes to follow in Larry Fitzgerald's footsteps—from ball boy to NFL star. I had a chance to mention Eric's goal to Larry a few seasons ago when the Colts were playing the Cardinals. He asked for my address and wrote a letter to Eric, which was still up on Eric's wall years later.

The content of the letter? Some thoughts about hard work, and a lot about the importance of getting an education. Larry exhorted

Eric to focus on his studies, to recognize that football's place in his life was temporary but that his education would stay with him forever. I really appreciate that Larry recognized that he was a role model for my son—and for stretching Eric in some very important directions by using that influence in a way that Eric wouldn't have anticipated. I don't know how much time it took out of Larry's day to write that letter, but I do know the impact it had, and continues to have, on my son.

Eric's dream is to play in the NFL someday, perhaps even on Larry Fitzgerald's team so he could be mentored by a great receiver. Maybe it will happen. In the meantime, I'm thrilled that Larry is using his platform as a role model for good. And I'm doubly blessed that he's using it for my son.

In this day and age, when so many of our country's children are growing up without a father in the home, I really appreciate the example that President Obama has become of fatherhood. Some people are surprised to hear me say that, because they don't agree with all the president's policies. Well, I don't agree with all his policies either. But to me, the images of the president with his wife and daughters, of having his mother-in-law living with them in the White House, convey that even though he's the president of the United States, his family is important to him. And I believe this is an important example to set, especially for African American children.

Part of the beauty of role models is that we can find them in unexpected places, at unexpected times. We also need to realize that we ourselves may be unexpected role models for others. In every

✧ **We can find role models in unexpected places, at unexpected times.**

interaction we have, someone is always watching us, and what we say and do forms a design for others to follow. As with President Obama and Larry Fitzgerald, we need to be aware that the impact we have on others might be for something totally different from what we anticipated.

How's that for pressure?

Speaking of pressure, I hear from time to time that I'm a role model for a number of young coaches. Sometimes my assistants would tell me that their friends in the league asked whether they really worked as few hours as rumored or if that was just another urban legend. It's not that we didn't work plenty of hours, they were able to assure their friends; we just tried to be smart about it and not spend time at the office just for the sake of spending time at the office so that someone would think we were doing a good job. We all know the amount of time spent is not necessarily an indicator of success. Now that I've retired from coaching, I can only hope that my former colleagues will carry on what they saw me model—working hard, but living a life in balance.

In my role as head coach for the Tampa Bay Buccaneers and Indianapolis Colts, I knew—whether I liked it or not—that the television cameras were often focused on me on the sidelines, especially during moments of high drama or at critical junctures in the game. I was always very sensitive to the example I set for others— other coaches, fans, parents, and children—in those situations. In my new role as a football analyst for NBC, I know that people are watching my mannerisms and body language and are listening not only to what I say but to how I say it. I hope I have always been a good role model for those who watch football; I can honestly say that I've tried to be.

+ **As a mentor leader, you must be aware that you are also a role model.**

As a mentor leader, you must be aware that you are also a role model. So live intentionally and remember that whatever settings you find yourself in, a lot of eyes will be on you, seeing things you don't even realize you're modeling.

DIRECT OPPORTUNITIES: MENTORING

Nobody made a greater mistake than he who did nothing because he could only do a little.

EDMUND BURKE

Wilbur Dungy. Allen Truman. Leroy Rockquemore. All were mentors of mine because they chose to be. Each one made a difference in my life through the platform God had given him—dad, "big brother," assistant principal.

I think we all should be looking for ways to improve, ways to grow. Mentors can help us do that, and we, in turn can help others the same way. Two of the greatest influences in our lives will be the people we associate with and the books or other media we read or watch. So, choose wisely.

I was fortunate, because even though I wasn't looking for other people to sharpen me, they came and found me anyway, time and time again. As a result, I feel a keen obligation, and have made it a priority, to focus outward on the people in my sphere of influence whom I can mentor.

Mentoring is a direct, one-on-one relationship. As such, it has the potential to cut into your time significantly. You can lead without mentoring, by choosing not to become engaged with your group; but mentor leadership requires a deliberate decision to get involved in someone else's life. So, no question, it takes time; but it will make an incredible difference in your organization and will establish a legacy that will pay dividends long after you're gone.

I was fortunate that Chuck Noll took me under his wing. He didn't have to. He could have let me figure things out for myself, and if I did, great, and if I didn't, he'd get someone else. Once again, though, I was blessed to come across a different type of coach. I was a young, inexperienced coach who was simply trying to learn what was expected of me, and I was overwhelmed at the prospect of coaching a veteran team like the Pittsburgh Steelers. Those same players had been my teammates just one year prior. And worse yet, they had been the ones teaching me the defense back then. Coach Noll, though, had patience and began teaching me how to teach football.

✦ **Mentor leadership requires a deliberate decision to get involved in someone else's life.**

He was always that way—with me and with others. I had played quarterback in high school and college, and I had no experience at all playing defense. Suddenly, when I played for the Steelers, I found myself on defense going up against the best football players in the world and learning on the fly. I made plenty of mistakes, believe me. I would often come off the field to find coaches yelling at me—quite often the passionate Bud Carson, who taught me so much. I remember a number of times when Bud would yell, "What are you doing! You are going to cost us the game if you keep that up. And before you can, I'll cut you! I'm not going to have Coach Noll fire me because of you—I'll get rid of you before he gets rid of me!"

And then Chuck Noll would come over. Never loquacious with the media, he would take his time with his players, always looking to teach us. During the heat of battle, he'd ask me what I was thinking and what I was looking at, and then he would take the time to teach me a better way to approach that particular situation. He helped me learn from my mistakes so they wouldn't happen again.

I don't think most people had an accurate perception of Chuck Noll. Because he was quiet, and because we were the Steel Curtain in a blue-collar town, I don't think people expected him to have an intentional, calm teaching approach.

In my experience with him, he seemed to take that approach with everyone. But I think that he probably took it a little further with me, especially when I became a coach myself. That's when he became even more directly involved in my development. He continued to teach me and give me the tools I needed to coach successfully, and as I came to understand and appreciate more of the system and what we were trying to accomplish, he would give me more responsibility. He was the consummate teacher, and he did all this with an intentional, direct style—leading, but always willing to walk beside me as a mentor leader.

I must admit I didn't realize what was happening at the time. When Chuck hired me as a coach, his wife, Marianne, told me that I was "one of Chuck's favorite players," which stunned me because he hadn't treated me any differently from anyone else on our team. He worked hard to make sure that, while he respected and nurtured the individual, he continually emphasized the overall good of the team and its mission first and foremost. It was then I began to realize that spending time one-on-one with individual coaches and players—growing them and nurturing them—wasn't contrary to a team-first approach. As a matter of fact, it caused the team concept to prosper. The time Chuck spent with individuals made the team grow stronger. As we all followed his example, it led to members of the team helping each other. Soon we had not only the coaches teaching, but also the veteran players teaching the younger guys.

Thomas Dimitroff is the general manager of the Atlanta Falcons. In his first two years with the team, Thomas has taken a measured and reasonable approach to his direct influence within the organization.

Before coming to the Falcons in 2008, he was director of college scouting for the New England Patriots. As he describes his first year as GM, he was scrambling to get his head above water and learn the various facets of the football business. Over the course of his first few months, he had to hire a new head coach and a complete coaching staff, prepare for free agency, and evaluate college talent for the upcoming draft. Thomas was mature enough and secure enough to lean on the experience of others around him on the

Falcons—people such as team president Rich McKay—as he negotiated that trial by fire.

By his second year on the job, he had a greater understanding of the football side of the business, but he continued to branch out to educate himself on the other aspects of the business, the non-football side, again relying on Rich McKay; Arthur Blank, the Falcons' owner; and others in the organization. Now, he said, he's looking to take others under his wing.

"Maybe I shouldn't have waited until now," he said, "but I did feel that I was trying to get my hands around what was going on. Now I need to start identifying others around me and nurturing their development in areas beyond their areas of responsibility so that they can lead the Falcons as well."

That's it. That's the direct influence we can all have. That's what a mentor leader does.

You don't have to be the head coach or general manager of a

+ **You don't have to be the head coach or general manager of a professional sports team to mentor someone.**

professional sports team to mentor someone. If you're a father, you have a sacred trust to mentor your children. If you're a husband or a wife—you're in. A friend—get going. An employer—what an opportunity! Maybe you're a teacher—well, you've heard my story about just one educator who understood his obligation as a mentor. The point is, anyone can be a mentor leader. And every mentoring opportunity comes with enormous potential significance, whether we see it at the time or not. Regardless of your style—deliberate or spontaneous—or your formal position within your organization, begin taking steps today to build into the lives of the people around you. It will improve your organization in the short term and over the long haul. And it might even have eternal significance.

ACTION STEPS

1. Name three mentors you have had. Stop and think about who they were, what their impact was in your life, and why they mentored you. How would your life be different if they had not taken the time to build into your life by mentoring you? Have you thanked them?

2. What did those mentors do well? What characteristics and qualities did they demonstrate that made their mentoring times with you effective? Can you implement those same qualities in your own life?

3. At a recent Impact for Living Conference, I encouraged the people in attendance to write a letter to their mentors, telling them how their lives had been affected. The feedback I received suggests that it's a worthy endeavor. People never grow tired of being told how they changed someone's life.

4. Don't forget that you are a role model—whether you want to be or not. Live as if your life is under constant scrutiny—because it is, by someone, somewhere.

5. What kind of role model will you be?

6. Are there special situations that God may have placed before you to act on? Has He provided the timing? Are you available? What are you waiting for?

7. Name three role models you have had. Were any of them people you knew directly? How did you incorporate lessons from their lives into your own life?

8. We all have God-given platforms. The size doesn't matter. What natural platforms do you have for influencing people's lives?

9. How can you become more sensitive to the unexpected moments when you can make a difference?

CHAPTER 6

THE MODEL OF A MENTOR LEADER: LIVING THE MESSAGE

Preach the gospel at all times; when necessary, use words.
ATTRIBUTED TO ST. FRANCIS OF ASSISI

You will be known by your words—and your actions. Jesus said, "It's not what goes into your mouth that defiles you; you are defiled by the words that come out of your mouth. . . . The words you speak come from the heart—that's what defiles you" (Matthew 15:11, 18).

Our words often betray what's inside us—our thoughts, motives, and attitudes. They are important because of the impact they have on the listener. But as important as our words are, what we *do* is even more critical. Think about how many times you've heard the following phrases: "Talk is cheap." "He talks the talk, but he doesn't walk the walk." "Actions speak louder than words." In our society, people often say one thing but do another. A quick review of the news headlines or the sports page will tell you that.

You will also be known by your faith. We all believe in something—even atheists do. But how passionately do you believe what you believe? In a world increasingly filled with people who are more pragmatic than committed, our faith will mark and define us for others to see—and follow. People are naturally drawn to believe in something larger than themselves, and they will follow someone whose life reflects a consistent commitment to higher values.

✛ **You will be known by what you model for others.**

Finally, you will be known by your heart. The commitments of your heart will write the legacy you leave to the world. Were you willing to get in the game and get your hands dirty to change a life? Were you crafting your eulogy by touching the lives of the people around you, the people who will miss you when you're gone? Your compassion for others is an indication of the attitude of your heart—and others will take notice.

In short, you will be known by what you model for others—through your words, your actions, your faith, and your heart.

For eternity.

KNOWN BY YOUR WORDS AND ACTIONS

What good is it, dear brothers and sisters, if you say you have faith but don't show it by your actions?

JAMES 2:14

You can tell the world who you are, but the you they see in action will be the you they remember.

It's a fact. That's how the world will know you. By your actions.

Who is the you that you want the world to see?

Who are you? Who do you want to be? Who *should* you be?

Who did God create you to be?

When you lead with words and actions consistent with God's

direction, you will add credibility to who you are. The Scripture above illustrates this timeless point, which is fleshed out more fully when you read the passage through verse 18:

> *What good is it, dear brothers and sisters, if you say you have faith but don't show it by your actions? Can that kind of faith save anyone? Suppose you see a brother or sister who has no food or clothing, and you say, "Good-bye and have a good day; stay warm and eat well"—but then you don't give that person any food or clothing. What good does that do?*
>
> *So you see, faith by itself isn't enough. Unless it produces good deeds, it is dead and useless.*
>
> *Now someone may argue, "Some people have faith; others have good deeds." But I say, "How can you show me your faith if you don't have good deeds? I will show you my faith by my good deeds."*

The truth about our faith can manifest itself in a variety of ways, most notably in how we act when we think no one is watching. Actions serve to demonstrate that our faith is at work. In my role as head coach, I was aware that my actions would be scrutinized, and I wanted them to reflect a godly perspective based on my understanding of God's Word. Especially in tough times, people will want to know if your actions measure up with your words and faith.

+ **Especially in tough times, people will want to know if your actions measure up with your words and faith.**

That wasn't my focus during my final year as head coach in Tampa Bay, or in other tough times I've experienced in life; but I've heard from other people, after the fact, that my actions had an impact on them because they saw me live what I had always professed.

During that final season with the Buccaneers, in 2001, I'm sure

I was under a microscope. Rumors were swirling from every conceivable corner that another coach was angling for my job, which fueled the uncertainty and the interest of the media and fans. Talk shows were constantly debating whether I should continue on as the head coach or be fired, beginning almost from the start of the preseason.

At least that's what I'm told. I didn't listen to the radio, and I didn't engage others in speculating about my job security. My only concern was to do the job I had right then—head coach of the Tampa Bay Buccaneers. I had long told my staff, the media, and others that my job was simply to coach. The team's owners would decide whether I would continue as their head coach. I knew that, but I believed that God would ultimately decide where I would be and what I would be doing. So I stayed focused on the present and away from the speculation.

Because I truly believed that my future was in God's hands, it was easy to reinforce my beliefs through my actions. I was truly at peace and was able to demonstrate that peace in the midst of the turmoil in what I did and what I said.

✦ **Leading through your words and actions tells the world who you are.**

Leading through your words and actions—whether someone's watching you or not—tells the world who you are, and more important, who you believe God created you to be. It not only is true in times of turmoil, but is woven throughout the very fabric of our lives.

James also reminds us of the destructive potential of our words, when he talks about the fickleness of the tongue:

Sometimes it praises our Lord and Father, and sometimes it curses those who have been made in the image of God. And so blessing and cursing come pouring out of the same mouth. Surely, my brothers and sisters, this is not right! Does a spring of water bubble out with both fresh water and bitter water?

Does a fig tree produce olives, or a grapevine produce figs? No, and you can't draw fresh water from a salty spring.

JAMES 3:9-12

In March 2009, Chicago Public Schools administrators proposed a new rule prohibiting high school coaches from using profanity while performing their coaching responsibilities. To my amazement, I was asked to go on a national radio show, not to debate whether this was a good rule, but to discuss whether it was even *possible* for coaches to comply. I assured the interviewer and the listeners that it certainly was possible and that I and many members of my staff were able to do it without need of an ordinance. I pointed out that the school board would be very disappointed if they went into the classrooms and found teachers cursing nonstop at the students and that I didn't understand why it should be any different on the playing field.

I believe that coaches, especially in high school, should be held to the same standard as classroom teachers—if not a higher one. I agree with the idea behind the proposed rule in Chicago, but I must say it's sad they would have to legislate such an obvious standard of leadership to those in powerful positions of influence with our youth. What message does that type of language send to those young people? That it's okay to demean someone if you're in charge? That it's okay for me to disrespect an official because I think he made a mistake?

+ Coaches should be held to the same standard as classroom teachers—if not a higher one.

In hearing stories of my father and the lessons he taught his children—and how he taught us those lessons—someone recently remarked that it must have been like being raised by a Christian

Confucius. My dad didn't use long stories like the parables of Jesus to make his points; instead, he relied on short statements—sound bites, if you will—that at times required far too much thought and contemplation for me to figure out.

One of those moments occurred when I was in junior high school and my father took me to a River Rouge High School basketball game to watch the legendary Lofton Greene in action. Coach Greene's success at River Rouge had become legendary in Michigan high school basketball.

River Rouge, Michigan, is an enclave of Detroit that was built up around a Ford Motor Company plant. It's about seventy miles east of Jackson, where I grew up. Coach Greene had been the head coach at River Rouge High School since 1943, and his teams had won twelve state titles in Class B (the second-largest classification in Michigan), including nine in an eleven-year period through the 1960s and early 1970s. In more than forty years of coaching in that auto-plant town, he built quite a dynasty, winning 739 games and coaching fathers and sons, uncles and nephews, brothers and cousins. Generation after generation, teaching commitment and passion. Teaching hard work, schoolwork, and teamwork. And, finally, even teaching a little about basketball.

My dad knew Coach Greene and had spoken about him on many occasions through the years. As a basketball fanatic, I knew about River Rouge and their success, of course; but until that game, I really didn't know much about the coach, other than what my dad had told me. When River Rouge came to Jackson, I was going to see some great players, but my dad wanted me to see their coach. It was an intentional teachable moment.

The hype from my dad—and he usually wasn't big on hyperbole—didn't live up to the experience. At first. The River Rouge team was truly a marvel to watch. They played fast. They moved the ball with precision on offense and ran a full-court press the entire game on defense. They were the proverbial "buzz saw" in slicing up Jackson's Lumen Christi Catholic High School that night.

Coach Greene? Truthfully? He was not that impressive to a junior high kid. He stayed in his seat for most of the game. He might as well have been a spectator, as far as I was concerned. He did get up during the time-outs and managed on a few occasions to talk to his team, but that was about all the coaching I saw from him. I was underwhelmed.

After the game, my dad asked me what I thought. I went on and on about what a tremendous team River Rouge had and how talented they were. They were incredibly good and completely synchronized in their actions.

"I wasn't very impressed with Coach Greene, though," I confessed. "He didn't do anything. He just sat there calmly with his arms folded. No expression. I didn't really see him do any coaching."

My dad offered one of his typical cryptic, Confucian one-liners: "When you're a teacher, you talk when you teach. You don't talk during the test."

I was about twelve and, not surprisingly, had no response to this. "If you teach well enough," he continued, "you really don't have to worry when the students are taking the test—they are prepared and can take care of themselves."

> ✛ When you're a teacher, you talk when you teach. You don't talk during the test.

I didn't give my father's words much thought for a number of years. As I progressed in sports through high school and college, most of the coaches I played for were high-energy guys who tried to control everything that happened on the court or field. They left no doubt that they were in charge, calling every play, reacting to every close call by an official, and generally coaching every minute of every game.

But the lesson my father tried to instill in me that night at the River Rouge–Jackson Lumen Christi basketball game wasn't lost on me forever. It wasn't until much later, sometime while I was in college at the University of Minnesota, that I suddenly remembered Coach Greene and thought that playing for a coach like him would be pretty appealing from a player's perspective. I filed it away with a new appreciation for his style. His actions during games reinforced completely his belief that he was a teacher of basketball, that he was teaching his players to understand the game and to be able to think for themselves on the court. They played fast because they knew what they were doing. I came to understand that Lofton Greene did a lot of coaching. You just had to be at practice to see most of it.

Nathan has a law school friend named David French, who had long argued in favor of military action in Iraq and was pleased when the United States took action in 2003. At the time, David was the head of an organization that protected the First Amendment rights of college students on both sides of the political aisle. One day, David called Nathan to inform him that he had applied to join the Judge Advocate General's Corps—the JAG Corps—which is the branch of the Army dealing with legal matters and military trials, as well as advising the military on any legal issues that may arise during the fighting of a war. For example, the issue of enhanced interrogation would likely come before members of the JAG Corps for their assessment. David explained that it had struck him one day that his words favoring military intervention felt hollow and demanded something more from him. "If it was important enough to send somebody else there, why wasn't it important enough for *me* to go?" Signing up for the military is not the right answer for everyone, he understood. But he felt increasingly compelled that it was what he was supposed to do.

He figured that his decision probably wouldn't ever directly affect his wife and two elementary-age children. As a thin, out-of-shape, thirty-seven-year-old Harvard Law graduate with a receding hairline, he was hardly what you would picture as Army material. However, much to his surprise, he passed every physical test and interview he faced and found himself attached to the Third Armored Cavalry

Regiment, based in Fort Hood, Texas. Within a year, he was in Diyala Province, Iraq, a stone's throw from Iran, making life-and-death decisions for himself and others as they rooted out al Qaeda from the surrounding villages.

Nathan asked David if that decision made sense in light of his commitment to his family back in Kentucky—he was in Iraq for almost a full year. And here I was, worried about my commute from Indiana to Florida for six months!

David paused. "Leaving them is not something I'm ecstatic about, to be sure. I'm sorry Nancy has to parent alone for a year—hopefully it's just a year." He was fully aware that the prior JAG officer attached to the Third Armored was in constant combat, and that other officers in that regiment had been killed in the last deployment. "But my kids do need to understand the importance of a call. If you're *called* to do something—committed to following through on your words—then sometimes, that is bigger than what we *want* to do. I hope my children grow up understanding that God may call them to do things that take them out of their comfort zone to benefit someone else."

> ✛ If you're *called* to do something, then sometimes, that is bigger than what we *want* to do.

Making sure that your actions back your words isn't usually a life-and-death enterprise, but it's every bit as important. What you do gives credibility to what you say, regardless of the setting. What you say and do is the person others will come to know. It is the *you* they will identify with when your name comes up or they see you in the distance or listen to you speak. The message of your words and actions will be the model of who you really are. Will that model be consistent with the model God had in mind when He created you?

As a person, as a parent, as a leader, do you espouse values of having a life, family, team, or organization that is consistent with your words and actions and in line with God's direction?

Are you leading your organization with long-term goals in mind that are in line with God's thoughts?

Make sure that your actions mirror your words. If they don't, there's no surer way to a credibility gap and resulting crisis of confidence for those who follow you.

Be the role model that God created you to be for others.

Be the message that He intended for you to be to all the world.

It may just be that someone needs that message, that model, that example at this very moment.

KNOWN BY YOUR FAITH

Our lives are a Christ-like fragrance rising up to God. . . .
And who is adequate for such a task?

2 CORINTHIANS 2:15-16

Faith. It undergirds it all. It is the foundation for everything else.

Faith is the essence and energy that empowers and encourages leaders to go on when they're not sure they can.

It is what drives us to look for potential in the lives of others and then compels us to build into those lives.

First and foremost, my faith is in God. The God who created all things. My faith is also in His Son, Jesus Christ, who sacrificed His life for me, and in the Holy Spirit, the helper sent to walk with us every day. I believe in other things as well, and all these beliefs guide and direct my leadership style.

I find it helpful to remember that people are watching me and how committed I am to the things I profess to believe, and whether those are worthy things. As I live my life, seeking to be a good role model and exercising mentor leadership, I hope that others can see my faith at work and have it affect their faith as well.

That's what happened with Naomi and Ruth in the Old Testament story I mentioned in chapter 4. Ruth, Naomi's daughter-in-law, was a Moabite, not a Jew. That's why Naomi encouraged Ruth to return to her family after her husband's death—so that she could marry someone from her own nation. However, during the ten years that Ruth had been married to Naomi's son, she had found the faith that Naomi had lived out in front of her a source of comfort and direction. In fact, Naomi's example of faith through difficult times had so affected Ruth that she had come to believe in God.

That Ruth was willing to leave her native land and follow Naomi unconditionally back to Bethlehem is evidence of the impact of Naomi's life as a role model. Ruth's knowledge of God came primarily through Naomi's example and witness, yet it was enough to compel Ruth to change the course of her life.

Here was Naomi, who had survived both the famine that had caused her and her family to leave their home in Bethlehem and then the subsequent death of her husband and her two sons, yet she still believed in God and that He was watching over her. Her faith was tested and stretched—but it remained unbroken.

And that message of her life changed another.

My faith was put to the test in a different sort of way in the 2006 AFC Championship Game against New England. The Patriots had won three of the last five Super Bowls and had knocked the Colts out of the playoffs in two of those seasons. Finally, we had them at home in Indianapolis, and we all felt it was our time to win, to finally reach our Super Bowl.

We promptly fell behind by eighteen points in the first half, and it would have been easy for our players to throw in the towel. No team had ever come back from that large a deficit in a championship game, but we had come back from similar deficits in other games. And because my players had seen me remain calm in those tough situations, they were willing to listen at halftime when I said, "It's still our time!"

It wasn't a frantic, desperate plea, but a calm assertion that we could win the game if we hung together and did what we were capable of doing. I believed that all those prior times when we had stayed calm in the face of adversity would pay off.

Faith.

Frankly, when you're in a crisis, it's too late to try to get people to follow you—unless you have already demonstrated faith and confidence in noncrisis times.

Our players believed. They executed the game plan, and we scored thirty-two points in the second half to win 38–34 and head to the Super Bowl for the first time since 1970 when the Colts were still in Baltimore.

> ✛ When you're in a crisis, it's too late to try to get people to follow you.

Remember, in times of crisis people will follow those with character. Not competence or authority, but *character*. It would be nice to have all three, of course, but if you have to choose which quality to build on, make sure you have an impeccable character. On that Colts team, we had leaders with character *and* faith.

As leaders mentoring others on the team and within the organization, our players would probably never have referred to themselves as ambassadors for their faith, but that is exactly what they were. They were known for their football ability, of course, but more important, in the context of being mentors and leaders, they were also known for their faith.

Faith will go a long way toward giving others a reason to follow you. Sometimes a demonstration of fervent belief is enough. David Hume, the eighteenth-century Scottish philosopher and scholar, was famously drawn to an example of faith. Though Hume was skeptical, at best, about many matters of religious faith, legend has it he was seen one morning hurrying off to hear George Whitefield, one of the best-known evangelists of the day. When Hume was asked if he was going to hear the charismatic Whitefield preach because he believed what Whitefield believed, he replied, "No, but *he* does!"

Whitefield seems to have had that effect on a lot of people. Benjamin Franklin, in his autobiography, tells of a time when he went to hear Whitefield speak and resolved not to contribute if the preacher took up a collection. However, Whitefield made such a compelling case for why his listeners should help the poor and needy that Franklin gave away all the money he had with him. Franklin adds that a friend of his was so moved by Whitefield's words that he tried to borrow money from others in the crowd in order to give it to the collection for the poor. It seems that reason, intellect, and resolve were no match for the passionate faith of George Whitefield.

Remember the story in Matthew 7:24-27 of the two men who built houses—one on sand and the other on rock? The houses were the same in all respects—except for the foundation. They looked the same, were built from the same materials, and provided the same shelter. For a while. Over time, however, the elements—adversity—tested the houses, and the differences appeared. The house on the rock stood firm, while the house on the sand was washed away. The house that survived was the one built on the foundation of faith in God.

Faith is the foundation and strength of the mentor leader, the guiding principle behind everything we do.

+ **Faith is the foundation and strength of the mentor leader.**

KNOWN BY YOUR LEGACY

Everybody can be great. Because anybody can serve. You don't have to have a college degree to serve. You don't have to make your subject and your verb agree to serve. . . . You don't have to know the second theory of thermodynamics in physics to serve. You only need a heart full of grace. A soul generated by love.

MARTIN LUTHER KING JR.

Mentor leaders will be known by their legacy.

The legacy we leave is a composite of the many things that guide the daily steps of the mentor leader.

Relationships. Impact. Involvement.

Character. Faith. Actions.

When all those traits combine with the mind-set of a mentor leader, lives *will* be changed for the better.

An excellent example of a leader who has built a strong legacy is Bob Hurley Sr., the legendary basketball coach at St. Anthony High School in Jersey City. In his career at St. Anthony, where he has coached since 1972, Hurley has amassed 974 victories and won 25 New Jersey state championships and 3 national championships. He is the father of former Duke All-American Bobby Hurley Jr. and the subject of the book *The Miracle of St. Anthony*—the true story of the coach and his St. Anthony basketball team, which has served as a ray of hope in the midst of the underprivileged neighborhood where the school is located. The story is also in development to be released as a movie by Walden Media.

Coach Hurley's goals and expectations for his players extended far beyond the basketball court. He saw his role and responsibility in their lives as much more than simply a basketball coach. Throughout his coaching career, he has also sought to be a mentor for each of his players. His goal was—and still is—to educate them about life well beyond the basketball court. He wants to point them toward successful, significant lives. Every day of his life, he continues to shape, develop, and write his legacy through the lives of his players, just as he's done for the last four decades. By influencing his players, other coaches, staff members, and teachers, he has succeeded in creating other mentor leaders.

One of Coach Hurley's players from the 1980s is former Notre Dame and NBA great David Rivers. Because Coach Hurley was involved in the lives of the Rivers family even after David Rivers had graduated, he knew about David's nephew Hank, who had joined a violent gang and made other poor decisions while growing up. Before Hank got to St. Anthony, he had already been incarcerated at age fourteen, and now, as an eighteen-year-old, he was looking at an eighteen-month prison sentence. Coach Hurley appeared before the court on Hank's behalf and appealed to the judge for leniency, telling him that he would take responsibility for the young man. He then took Hank under his wing, but made it clear to him that there was no margin for error. None.

Hank stayed out of trouble, graduated from high school, and went on to attend Stephen F. Austin State University. He is now playing professional basketball overseas. In *The Miracle of St. Anthony*, Hank said, "If I never met Coach Hurley, I don't know where I'd be. Actually, I do know: either coming or going to prison. Or I'd be dead. He was the best thing to ever happen to me. He taught me a work ethic, taught me leadership, taught me to live your life the right way."*

✢ Every day of his life, Coach Hurley continues to shape, develop, and write his legacy through the lives of his players.

Coach Bob Hurley Sr. is a shining example of a mentor leader in action, building a positive legacy of changed lives by pouring his life into the lives of others.

My mother is another person who is known by the legacy she has built. As a teacher in Jackson, she was one of the best I've ever seen at making sure that people were given every chance to make the most of themselves. She simply refused to let her students settle for less than their best. I've told the story before about a student who had spent his entire childhood in the special-education track of the Jackson schools. But when he landed in one of my mother's classes and she realized that he had been misdiagnosed, she became his advocate and

---

*Quoted in Adrian Wojnarowski, *The Miracle of St. Anthony* (New York: Penguin, 2005), 304.

wouldn't give up until he had been moved back into regular classes. That student went on to graduate from college and is yet another example of the power of mentor leadership.

A life changed.

That's simply how my mother was.

That's how we should be too. Looking for lives to change and hearts to impact, that we might model the message of the mentor leader, leaving a legacy of changed lives and a better world, day by day, one life at a time.

ACTION STEPS

1. Consider your legacy. You can *tell* the world who you are, but the you they hear and see in action will be the you they remember. What kind of legacy are you building?

2. Evaluate your consistency. Do your actions mirror your words? There is no surer way to create a credibility gap than if they don't.

3. Examine your words. What comes out of your mouth reveals the condition of your heart. What do your words reveal about your thoughts, motives, and attitudes?

4. Evaluate your faith. Does your faith create a foundation that others can believe in? Are you building on sand or on solid rock?

CHAPTER 7

THE MEANS OF A MENTOR LEADER: MAXIMIZING TEAM PERFORMANCE

The secret is to work less as individuals and more as a team.
As a coach, I play not my eleven best, but my best eleven.

KNUTE ROCKNE

You can achieve more with a team than without. I've seen it time and again: A team that is functioning well is more than just the sum of its parts. In fact, the Colts team that won the Super Bowl in 2007 was not the most talented team I had during my years in Indianapolis. But it was the team that came together best and played at a higher level than you might have expected from the sum of its individual pieces. Each member of the organization had bought into our clear vision and the way we planned to accomplish it, both on and off the field. Team members accepted their roles and saw the roles of others as valuable. Together they encouraged and assisted each other in bringing their best to the cause.

The same is true in other areas of endeavor. We have all seen organizations that have foundered and not lived up to expectations, despite talented individuals. But I have seen numerous organizations accomplish much greater outcomes when each piece is functioning well within the whole.

To maximize team performance, the leaders must create the appropriate culture: a culture that underscores the mission, vision, and values of the organization. A healthy culture values its people.

✛ **To maximize team performance, the leaders must create the appropriate culture.**

Great organizations aren't great places to work simply by chance—they are intentionally created.

An organization that values employees will work to understand and appreciate the differences among people. Diversity is not something we should merely accept as a legal mandate. Rather, we should recognize that our diverse backgrounds and life experiences enhance the synergy of a high-performing team.

Efficient, high-performing teams create a level of camaraderie. It isn't necessary that all teammates become the best of friends, but a level of respect and appreciation will characterize teams that are truly maximizing their output.

For maximum achievement and sustainability, it helps to view your followers as *volunteers*, which requires a different approach from the authoritarian or autocratic leadership that used to characterize many organizations. That high-control management style might be appropriate in certain situations, but I don't believe that type of leadership has a long shelf life.

Jim Collins speaks of getting the right individuals "on the bus" in his classic book *Good to Great*. He's right. It doesn't take stars. It takes the right people in the right positions to build a successful team.

When a leader creates an appropriately healthy, stimulating, and nurturing culture and is dedicated to mentoring people, valuing them, and giving them the tools to succeed, the organization's vision and mission are not only achievable but also sustainable.

CREATING A CULTURE

The great law of culture is: Let each become all that he was created capable of being.

THOMAS CARLYLE

In the week after the Tampa Bay Buccaneers fired me in 2001, I received a number of phone calls. One of the most intriguing was from Jim Irsay, the owner of the Indianapolis Colts. He not only wanted me to coach the Colts, he wanted me to help build an organization that stood for something beyond football. He wanted a team that emphasized character, values, and family, and he wanted the organization to extend itself in meaningful ways into the community. The first time Jim and I spoke, we didn't talk about football at all. Instead, we talked about values and priorities. He wanted to change the culture of the Colts organization, believing that establishing the right values and the right approach would make us a better team and improve our chances of being successful, both on and off the field. He had long admired the way the Rooney family ran the Pittsburgh Steelers, and he wanted to build an excellent program, as they had, that would also win championships.

Jim Irsay's vision and mission intrigued me more than the thought of simply coaching another team, so my family and I headed to Indiana to begin the next phase of our lives. Over the next seven years, the Colts enjoyed many of the fruits of those efforts. Together as an organization, we formed an entity that stood for more than the simple goal of winning a Super Bowl. Although that was one of our goals, to be sure, we were clear that our mission as an organization incorporated far more than merely winning on the field. I told our coaches, players, and staff that if all we did was win a Super Bowl, we would fall far short of our potential and accomplish far less than Jim Irsay had in mind when he hired me.

The culture you create permeates everything you touch. The culture we developed in the Colts organization during those seven years carried us through some difficult times and allowed us to be successful as citizens in the community. The culture we instilled—which became the fabric of the organization—outlined for everyone how we would treat people within the organization—players, coaches, owners, administrators, everyone who was part of our family. It set the standard by which we as individuals and as an organization would partner with our community. The kind of culture I am talking about places value on people, no matter the brightness of their "star power."

> ✦ **The culture you create permeates everything you touch.**

I know some coaches who, during the season, would turn over the bottom end of their rosters—those marginal players whose talent was more easily replaced—by bringing in other players who were currently on the street. They did it to send a message to their players that they had better continue to work hard or they could be replaced. The question is, are you really sending a message to a star player who isn't working hard by cutting a less talented player who is doing everything he's been asked? Many times these moves would have the opposite effect to what the coach intended. Instead of motivating players to work harder, it caused them to question how hard they wanted to work for an organization that treated some of its hardest workers so shabbily.

Of course, every team in the NFL is constantly looking for players who will make them better, and if necessary we would make a roster move if we found someone who could improve us as a team. We'd also make moves for nonperformance, character issues, or if injuries forced us to pick up a player to fill a position.

But that's different from stirring up the roster simply to keep the players on edge and motivated. I would never do that—simply to watch others squirm and struggle to keep their spots on the team or to have to uproot their families in midseason after being cut loose. That's not the kind of culture I wanted.

Some coaches value fear as part of the fabric of their organizations. But that's not how I do things. For me, once I've preached family and significance and making a difference, then I have to make decisions—*all* of them—with that as a backdrop. If we were indeed a family, as I had said we were, then I needed a pretty good reason for turning over those bottom roster spots. I couldn't do it just to do it. Adding an element of "hunger" or "insecurity" to our culture would not complement what we were trying to accomplish and what we stood for as an organization. Instead, it would run counter to the culture we had set out to create—a culture that valued people, how they were treated, and how together we could impact the world.

Keli McGregor, the president of the Colorado Rockies who died suddenly in April 2010, was a friend of mine. During his seventeen years with the Rockies, he took an approach similar to mine in crafting a vision for his organization. The Rockies' mission statement captures Keli's approach in the profound simplicity of its words:

> The mission of the Colorado Rockies Baseball Club is to embody the principles and practices of a championship organization in both the sport and business of baseball. In the rich tradition that has made baseball America's pastime, we are committed to conduct our business with integrity, service, quality, and trust.

Note that the mission statement says nothing about winning the World Series. It doesn't mention winning the division or the league pennant, or even making the playoffs. Yet the Rockies have had two spectacular seasons in the last three: a 2007 National League pennant, which resulted in a World Series appearance; and a 2009 playoff appearance. They also had some lean years before those. But either way, their on-field performance was not their primary marker for measuring the success of the Colorado Rockies organization.

Their vision has allowed them to treat their employees and their community with the respect that each deserves, creating value for both. It encompasses the work of everyone in the organization, whether directly related to the on-field product or not. They have redefined their bottom line by expanding it well beyond the financial to include the health and well-being of everyone who has a stake in the community partnership known as the Colorado Rockies Baseball Club.

✣ **Their vision has allowed them to treat their employees and their community with the respect that each deserves.**

For example, in implementing their mission statement, the Rockies have built well over one hundred Little League fields throughout the state of Colorado, and they treat their stadium and ball club as a public trust. They regularly partner in projects with local charities, the city of Denver, and the county, and they provide valuable support and encouragement for the people of Colorado. At an Impact for Living conference in 2009, where Keli and I were both presenters, he told me that several years ago, the Rockies had given each member of the organization a bottle of champagne at the start of the year, representing the on-field championship they anticipated would eventually accompany their off-field success.

Finally, in 2007, when they achieved their goal of winning the National League crown, they celebrated as a unit—players, coaches, and office staff. In a ring ceremony that included every member of the organization, from the club president to a possible future Hall of Fame outfielder to the housekeeping staff, each person received an identical ring. "We were going to celebrate reaching the vision," Keli said. "We had all earned it. No one was less vital to reaching it, and they knew it." And in so many ways, the Rockies made sure that everyone in the organization knew that to be true.

The significance of vision was known long before professional sports franchises began examining it and realizing its importance in achieving desired outcomes. Nearly a century ago, Theodore Roosevelt said, "We need leaders of inspired idealism, leaders to whom are granted great visions, who dream greatly and strive to make their dreams come true; who can kindle the people with the fire from their own burning souls."*

Chuck Noll was very clear on this point. His aim was to create a specific culture in everything he did and in the way he did it— the Steeler Way. A player didn't have to be the biggest, fastest, or strongest at his position, and a coach didn't have to be the smartest or most creative, as long as everyone bought in to the Steeler Way. Coach Noll believed that our culture in Pittsburgh was unique, and he wanted people who would stick with the program and not try to implement ideas from other NFL clubs. One of the reasons we were able to win four Super Bowls in the 1970s was that every Steeler believed and bought into the team culture. And three decades later, the Steeler Way is still working—and winning—in Pittsburgh.

Coach Noll was an important part of that culture, but he also had the complete backing of the owners, as I did in my relationship with Jim Irsay in Indianapolis. Art Rooney Sr., the founder of the Steelers, was an indispensable component of the culture as well. Could Chuck Noll have created the Steeler Way without the wholehearted support of Mr. Rooney? Maybe, but it wouldn't have been easy. There would have been continual tension, longer meetings, and more explaining to do about why things should be done a certain way. Realistically, the culture

---

*James M. Strock, *Theodore Roosevelt on Leadership* (Roseville, CA: Forum, 2001), 166.

known as the Steeler Way could not have been developed without Mr. Rooney's support. The fundamental keys to the culture of any organization can only be achieved when everyone is on the same page.

When I joined the Steelers, Mr. Rooney still lived in the same inner-city Pittsburgh house he had always lived in. He walked to work each day, reflecting the blue-collar values of a blue-collar town. When the Steelers went to the Super Bowl, he refused the limousine customarily provided for team owners and did what he always did when traveling with the team—he rode the team bus or called a cab.

At the other end of the spectrum, I know a public relations director of a professional sports team who lost his job, in part because he failed to use *all* the various titles of one of the team's executives in a publicity release. That kind of thing would never have happened with the Steelers. Mr. Rooney's humble example left an indelible impression on anyone who ever worked for him, including me.

The people of Pittsburgh knew that Art Rooney cared about them and their well-being. For that and many other reasons, everyone viewed the Steelers as a community trust under the stewardship of the Rooneys. What Mr. Rooney demonstrated day after day—at the office, in his neighborhood, and in the larger community of Pittsburgh—was an authentic and sincere respect for everyone he came in contact with. Alongside Chuck Noll, he built a culture that will outlive both of them—a culture that allowed his son and successor, Dan Rooney, to accept the position of U.S. ambassador to Ireland in 2009, knowing that the Pittsburgh Steelers were still operating the Steeler Way.

I don't think it's an accident that the New England Patriots, under owner Robert Kraft and head coach Bill Belichick, have had so much success over the past decade. Like Art Rooney and Chuck Noll, they have done a great job of creating a culture and getting people from diverse backgrounds and football experiences to buy into their team-first mentality.

Sports franchises are not the only kind of organization in which culture is important. Think of General Electric and the culture of leadership they developed in years past. Despite being an enormous conglomerate—a business model that has fallen out of favor in many ways—GE has provided tremendous shareholder value and innovative products. That kind of success doesn't happen without great leadership, a fact noted in a 2005 *Fortune* magazine article: "When a company needs a loan, it goes to a bank. When a company needs a CEO, it goes to General Electric, which mints business leaders the way West Point mints generals."* At one point that year, five of the thirty companies whose stocks make up the Dow Jones Industrial Average were headed by former executives from GE.

Why does GE's culture foster the development of leadership? Certainly there are costs to GE, both in terms of developing that talent and of having it walk out the door—sometimes to a competitor. But I think that culture has also led to GE's sustained success. As talent leaves, the company simply continues to develop new leaders. With all those up-and-coming leaders scattered throughout the company, it can't help but increase results within the company.

GE's very intentional focus on leadership development has also, I believe, attracted more potential leaders to GE than the company might otherwise have had. Once it gained a reputation for developing leaders, it had to have become a magnet for bright young people looking to maximize their leadership potential.

Will the results always work out for the leaders who leave? No. Just as GE has a culture in which these leaders were developed, the companies they move on to have cultures in place to which the new leaders must be able to adapt and adjust.

---

*Ellen Florian Kratz, "Get Me a CEO from GE!" *Fortune* (18 April 2005).

The same is true within the NFL. I was fortunate during my coaching career to have been surrounded by bright, talented leaders, and I tried to build into their lives as much as I could. Sometimes they ended up leaving and finding great success within a new organization, as Mike Tomlin did when he became the head coach of the Pittsburgh Steelers in 2007. Mike no doubt benefited from the culture in Pittsburgh, which still embraces the same qualities I learned there and exported to the Tampa Bay Buccaneers and Indianapolis Colts. Other times, a coach may go to an organization whose culture and entrenched interests end up being a poor fit, despite everyone's best efforts and intentions.

Other organizations provide a successful, healthy, encouraging, and uplifting culture without directly focusing on leadership like GE. But these corporate cultures are still based on the companies' core values. Take Google, for example, a company that emphasizes the importance of being together and being a member of the team. At Google, you'll find very few cubicles or closed offices. Instead, they have a lot of open space and open cafeteria seating. They also installed break rooms with foosball and pool tables, and areas with volleyball courts, allowing people who don't work together to interact. One of the company's stated values is the importance of having ideas shared across working groups. The open spaces and informal gatherings reinforce that value at every turn. It happens naturally as part of the culture.

+ **If you want to develop mentor leadership, you must foster a culture that supports it.**

An organization's culture, whether at Google, GE, or the Indianapolis Colts, doesn't create leadership, but it reinforces the focus on leadership, allowing it to develop organically, yet intentionally.

If you want to develop mentor leadership, you must foster a culture that supports it. Get the culture right, and you're on your way.

DIVERSITY ENHANCES EXCELLENCE

There are different kinds of spiritual gifts, but the same Spirit is the source of them all. There are different kinds of service, but we serve the same Lord. God works in different ways, but it is the same God who does the work in all of us.

I CORINTHIANS 12:4-6

Mentor leaders are always looking to add the right pieces, the right skill sets, and the right mix of diversity to the organization. Differences among the team will enhance its drive for success, if handled properly within the context of the culture, vision, mission, and values of the organization. God created us each with different talents, abilities, and strengths. We are also unique in our life experiences, outlooks, and personalities. Because of our differences, we will excel in different ways. Some things that are simple or obvious to me won't be for you, and vice versa. It's the combination of our diverse strengths that makes the team stronger.

✢ **Mentor leaders are always looking to add the right pieces, the right skill sets, and the right mix of diversity to the organization.**

There have been many great coaches in the history of the NFL and college football. Some have been master tacticians or great strategists, while others have not. Though mastery of the Xs and Os is definitely a part of the game, it isn't the primary characteristic of the all-time great coaches. Instead, what sets them apart is their ability to reach across a variety of backgrounds to get everyone on the same page.

Getting everyone to pull in the same direction is not always easy, but it is possible to reach across diverse backgrounds to do it. Obviously, I had more in common with some of my players than I did with others, but I needed to be able to relate with *all* of them at some level. Later in my career, I learned that I needed to be creative. As I've mentioned,

I hired some coaches with an eye toward their youth, while others I brought in for their extensive experience. I also talked with my son Eric, who was close in age to some of the players, to get a sense of what would connect more readily with the younger players.

On all the essential and core issues—our mission, vision, and values—I required unity. No compromise could be tolerated there. For example, I wasn't going to tolerate certain behaviors or guys who felt they didn't have to be accountable to me or their teammates. However, in areas where I could be more flexible—the nonessential issues, such as music in the weight room, movies on the team's plane, attire—I learned to give the players room for diversity.

Okay, so how do you do this? How can you learn to be flexible and deal with diversity, to see others who aren't like you in a way that allows you to meet them where they are and to help them become all they can be?

How can you accept people from differing backgrounds and foster their growth without abandoning your own culture and beliefs? How do you value people who are different just as much as you value those who are similar to you?

For me, the answers lie in the Bible.

In Acts 1:8, Jesus posed a leadership challenge to His followers. Just before He ascended to heaven, He said, "You will be my witnesses, telling people about me everywhere—in Jerusalem, throughout Judea, in Samaria, and to the ends of the earth." For His followers, staying in Jerusalem made sense. But to go into the other two areas—Samaria and the ends of the earth (that is, the non-Jewish world)—would be a radical departure from "the way we've always done it." For centuries, the Jews had been told to avoid the people of other nations. Now Jesus was telling His followers to seek out foreigners—to go to them, bringing the message of salvation. And as you would expect from a good mentor leader, Jesus had already modeled for them what He meant.

There's a wonderful story of boundary-busting, cross-cultural outreach recorded in the Gospel of John, chapter 4. Jesus, on a journey from Judea to Galilee, had to go through Samaria, a region inhabited by a people of mixed heritage whom the Jews despised. Around noon, Jesus and His followers came to the town of Sychar, and while the others went into town to get some food, Jesus, tired and thirsty, sat down by a well to rest. When a Samaritan woman approached, Jesus asked her for a drink of water and engaged her in conversation.

There was just one problem—that wasn't accepted behavior. No self-respecting Jewish man would have dared to be caught in that situation: speaking to a Samaritan woman, in broad daylight and in public. But Jesus wasn't concerned with social convention. He knew what the woman truly needed, and He offered her healing and wholeness and sent her on her way to live a new and better life.

+ **We must reach beyond the boundaries that separate us and connect with people who are different from us.**

Jesus was all about crossing over and reaching beyond the boundaries we establish based on our differences. In the example He set for His followers, Jesus knocked down the barriers—of culture, ethnicity, gender, faith, and age, among others—that we allow to separate us from other people. To be effective mentor leaders, we must do what Jesus taught us to do: We must reach beyond the boundaries that separate us and connect with people who are different from us.

It's important to note that Jesus didn't just tell His followers the plan and then send them out to implement it. Rather, He spent three years educating and equipping them first. We might glean any number of principles from the lessons Jesus taught His disciples, but I want to emphasize three in particular that apply to our role as mentor leaders:

- *Truly value others*, which is at the heart of Jesus' command to "love your neighbor as yourself" (Matthew 22:39; Mark 12:31).
- *Don't see yourself as above service*, as Jesus told James, John, and the other disciples: "Whoever wants to be a leader among you must be your servant" (Mark 10:43).
- *See yourself as an ambassador for God*, doing something for the simple reason that it's the right thing to do, not for expediency or gain. "We are Christ's ambassadors; God is making his appeal through us. We speak for Christ when we plead, 'Come back to God!'" (2 Corinthians 5:20).

Jesus surrounded Himself with the right people—a group with different personalities, strengths, and abilities—and cast a vision for them. He got involved in their lives and taught them how to be the leaders He would need in the organization He was setting up—the Kingdom of God. I believe you would agree that what He set up has had staying power.

With the right focus—on the vision and mission—diverse experiences, backgrounds, and ethnicities are not something to be feared, but rather something to be embraced as a sure way to maximize the performance of the team.

Tampa Bay Steel is run by founder Buck McInnis and president Mark Dillon with a very diverse workforce, including on matters of faith. They employ roughly 150 people, including management executives, sales representatives, truck drivers, cutters, welders, and others who process and distribute tens of millions of dollars' worth of steel annually. Buck and Mark are unabashed about their management style—leading through biblical principles. For example, in accordance with the Golden Rule, found in Matthew 7:12, to do unto others as you would have them do unto you, Mark decided to begin paying his suppliers more quickly, holding his company to the same standards it applies to its customers.

Mark told me that everyone knows where Buck stands as the founder of the business and how he makes his decisions. They know the expectations Buck has placed on the company and its long-term vision. At the same time, Buck embraces the diversity of the organization by meeting and engaging every employee where he or she is and by creating a culture that recognizes both the reality and the benefit of different experiences and beliefs.

In this day and age, it's not possible—nor would it be desirable—to staff an organization or a team with people who are just like you. Mark and Buck can't hire an all-Christian staff or one that shares their level of education, political mind-set, or charitable inclinations. And they shouldn't *want* to hire that way. Diverse experiences and perspectives bring so much more to the team. Of course, they also bring challenges for the leader, requiring a willingness to listen, to learn and understand, and to be flexible—things that are already within the mind-set of a mentor leader.

Joe Marciano, my special teams coordinator with the Tampa Bay Buccaneers, was a bachelor who believed he was called to adopt a child. He spoke to me about it before embarking down that path. I'm glad he felt he could approach me about it, because it opened up the lines of communication. Joe was able to proceed not only with my blessing, but also with the understanding that we would do whatever was possible as an organization to ease his transition into fatherhood.

When Joe successfully adopted, he needed to have steady help around his house for his new son, but he didn't want to be an absentee father. Joe and I worked out our meeting times so that he could meet individually with me in the afternoons and go home right after practice. We provided a tape machine for him to have at his house so that, after he had spent some time with his son in the evening and gotten him settled for bed, Joe could watch the tape he would normally see at the office. Joe's work schedule, outside of our practices and his morning special-teams meetings, could be adjusted, and it was worth the effort it took to work out an accommodation to meet his individual needs.

The adjustments we made had no impact at all on our chances to win. But they did provide a man who desperately wanted to be a dad the opportunity to nurture and grow with his young son. All it took was a little communication, some creative thought, and a willingness to be flexible.

As a mentor leader, you are already working to understand the people who are following you, so the diversity you find will ultimately play into your strengths as you continue down this path. Embracing diversity in the nonessentials will strengthen and enrich your organization.

TOGETHER—ALWAYS MOVING FORWARD

A person standing alone can be attacked and defeated, but two can stand back-to-back and conquer. Three are even better, for a triple-braided cord is not easily broken.

ECCLESIASTES 4:12

Every team member is important to the whole, yet the team can move on without any individual. "Important but not indispensable" is how Coach Noll put it.

He used to say, "We need every man on this roster to win, but no player is so important that we can't win without him." He encouraged everyone to work hard because each one's contributions were valuable, but no single player was the primary reason for our success. Coach Noll kept everyone motivated, yet he had a great way of keeping everything in perspective.

It was a tough balancing act, but he managed it well. His words and his actions were consistent. We knew that if one of our star players was injured, we could still play well as a team and win. Even though our roster was full of future Hall of Famers, our games were never about individual accomplishments. Teamwork was valued above all. It was always about the combined efforts of individuals who were melding their strengths into something we called the Pittsburgh Steelers.

What we achieved we achieved together. As a result, no one was ever left to think that he was the most important piece of the puzzle. Instead, every piece was important and necessary to accomplish our goals. Over the years, I've found that "important but not indispensable" is a much healthier and less pressurized way to view myself.

> ✛ I've found that "important but not indispensable" is a much healthier and less pressurized way to view myself.

I always felt that Coach Noll's real genius as a leader was his ability to develop great skills and leadership qualities in individual players, while at the same time helping us to realize that we were greater together than we could ever be apart.

Too many leaders give lip service to the collective power and impact of the organization, but then continue to stockpile high performers without regard to whether those individuals will complement the other members of the team.

Bill Belichick, on the other hand, is one who has a knack for bringing in star players from other teams, even players who had trouble fitting in with their previous teams, and getting them to realize that team success is of utmost importance. Many of these stars have had smaller individual roles with New England, but they've enjoyed more collective success. Even though the Patriots were our bitter rivals when I was with the Colts, I always admired Coach Belichick's ability to create that type of team spirit.

If you and your team are truly in it together, you won't find yourself in the situation where it's "my way or the highway." As we've discussed, mentor leaders are always willing to learn and grow, seeking advice and guidance as they lead others and help them develop. When done right, mentor leadership is an ongoing process of leading and being led, of developing ourselves and developing future leaders. My dad always told me that the two easiest ways to grow were to listen to other people and to read. Listening has definitely come easier for me than reading, but as I've gotten older I've seen the value of reading, too. So many times I've found a valuable nugget that has really helped me from a book or an article that someone passed on to me.

C. S. Lewis figured it out long before I did. In *The Voyage of the Dawn Treader*, the third book of his Chronicles of Narnia, which was written to illustrate matters of life and faith, Lewis mentions the critical tie between books and life. In a climactic scene in which Eustace confronts a dragon but doesn't know what it is, Lewis interjects, "Edmund or Lucy or you would have recognized it at once, but Eustace had read none of the right books."

Our world is rapidly changing and complex. New ideas and situations come flying at us. Are we able to adjust and adapt, to learn and grow and be prepared? If we're not sure, then we must read to broaden our understanding and deepen our knowledge. Even if we think we have a handle on things, we should read anyway.

We also need to listen to and engage with others as we embark on the path of mentor leadership. Success is something we will achieve *together*.

✛ **Success is something we will achieve *together*.**

When I arrived in Tampa Bay as a first-time head coach, I had my training camp rooming assignment plan already worked out. We would select roommates in alphabetical order. Simply line up the roster by last name, pair them up, and send them off. It was easy, clean, and I wanted to start building the culture. It would help send the message that we were all equal parts of a unified team. It was the right idea to promote, and most of the teams I had coached had done it that way.

Before I could announce my plan, general manager Rich McKay took me aside. "It's not going to work, Tony," he said. I assured him that it would—we'd done it this way before.

"You've never had Warren Sapp on your roster. You don't want to room him with Mark Royals or Al Singleton or whoever would be next to him alphabetically. You just don't. The only guy who rooms with Warren is Derrick Brooks. Anyone other than Brooks with Sapp will be a disaster."

Rich wasn't trying to throw cold water on my plans, and he wasn't just trying to show me that he was in charge. He was trying to help me. In this case, he had experience that I did not, experience from which I could benefit if I was smart.

I took Rich's words to heart and altered my plans slightly, heeding the words of Proverbs 15:22: "Plans go wrong for lack of advice; many advisers bring success."

How we respond to advice, correction, and constructive criticism makes all the difference:

Mockers hate to be corrected,
so they stay away from the wise.
A glad heart makes a happy face;
a broken heart crushes the spirit.
A wise person is hungry for knowledge,
while the fool feeds on trash.
PROVERBS 15:12-14

Of course, there are also times for courage and standing your ground. I'm not suggesting that you capitulate every time someone offers a contrary view. If, however, someone offers constructive input, you would be arrogant not to at least consider it.

It's all part of the journey—together.

LEAD VOLUNTEERS FOR EXTRAORDINARY ACHIEVEMENT

The mercenaries will always beat the draftees, but the volunteers will crush them both.

CHUCK NOLL

Ordinary effort and processes will lead to ordinary results if people are working only as individuals, or merely working *alongside* each other, rather than working *with* each other.

To achieve extraordinary results, you need a team of people doing ordinary things in a way that complements one another's efforts. Working together is what leads to exceptional results.

One of the best ways to get people to work together is to prepare as if you will be leading a team of volunteers. A good friend of mine realized the power and potential of that approach a few years ago as he was preparing to serve a term as the governor of the Florida Kiwanis clubs. The people he would be working with truly were volunteers, as Kiwanis is one of the world's largest philanthropic volunteer organizations. My friend would have to energize and unify 16,000 club members scattered throughout the state, their 350 club presidents, more than 10,000 high school Key Club members, and more than 1,000 members of Circle K in colleges within the state.

> ✛ One of the best ways to get people to work together is to prepare as if you will be leading a team of volunteers.

A tall order under any circumstances.

To get the results that everyone was hoping for—fulfilling the Kiwanis mission statement of "serving the children of the world"—he realized that it was going to take significant buy in from everyone. He also realized that, as volunteers, they didn't *have* to do anything he suggested. He couldn't dock their pay or fire them. And he didn't want to create an environment that would cause people to walk away.

Instead, he realized that he had to continue to cast the vision of the need Kiwanis was trying to address and paint a picture by *persuasion*, rather than fiat, that would energize others to go beyond what might ordinarily be expected.

Even though Kiwanis is a volunteer organization, he found that people were usually willing to go beyond what they had signed up to do—much like in the workplace when people rally around a compelling vision. But to meet the extraordinary needs of the children Kiwanis was serving, they would need to go well beyond what they were "supposed to do," beyond what was expected, because the lives of the children they were called to serve hung in the balance.

If you are trying to get the people you lead to go above and beyond their simple job descriptions, you must make sure they understand the ultimate organizational goal—your vision and mission—and believe in its importance until it becomes shared by all. Wherever you can, you need to "put a face" on what you are talking about.

I would venture to say that if you asked the thirty-two National Football League general managers or presidents to define their organizational mission, the most popular answer by far would be "to win the Super Bowl." That mission is a tangible goal for the fifty-three players on the active roster and all the coaches, but what about other people in the organization? What in that mission statement will inspire them to do more than simply punch the time clock, put in an honest day's work, and go home? For example, if I'm the receptionist and our mission is to win the Super Bowl, does it really matter how pleasant I am when I answer the phone?

When Weeb Ewbank was head coach of the New York Jets, he reportedly answered a question about his mission by saying, "My job is to sell tickets." That response actually creates more organizational energy than the goal of winning a Super Bowl, because selling tickets involves everyone in the organization—including the receptionist, whose phone-answering demeanor might affect a potential ticket buyer's perception of the organization. Selling tickets involves not only the ticketing department but also football operations and coaching, marketing, community relations, and public relations—since the club's image will affect that goal as well. I'm not suggesting that selling tickets is the best possible mission for a team, but it does serve to illustrate the importance of articulating a vision and mission that everyone in the organization can buy into.

✦ **By focusing on persuasion instead of position or authority, you will begin to capture the hearts of the people you lead.**

Viewing the members of your organization as volunteers—and really, they aren't far from it, given how transient the workforce is these days—forces you to see them in a different light. You'll begin to lead in ways that demonstrate respect and appreciation. By focusing on persuasion instead of position or authority, you will move beyond fear or "the power of the paycheck" as motivators and begin to capture the hearts of the people you lead. They will recognize and appreciate your genuine concern for their welfare and growth—all of which will benefit the organization.

You must get to know the members of your team and learn how to energize them before you can expect them to buy into a common mission. You have to be able to explain the mission in terms they can understand and persuade them that it is worth pursuing. It isn't enough to say, "Here's the plan; get on board." The members of your organization want to embrace the mission in a way that lets them not only share in it but also own it and have a stake in the outcome. Simply put, you have to make it mean more to them than just a paycheck.

I have a friend who came out of retirement to lead a troubled health care insurer a few years back. The company was under federal investigation and had lost some of its insurance lines to regulatory issues. It was facing the reality of having to lay off employees for the lines that no longer existed, and the remaining employees were going to have to do more, in many instances, for less compensation. Other insurers were already beginning to approach the company's employees, draining the firm of the talent it needed to survive.

My friend embarked on a national tour of the company's four offices—which employed more than two thousand people—and explained the new landscape to them. He said he realized early on that the message was fairly bleak—work more for less with no guarantee of survival—but that the message did provide an incentive: saving their jobs. However, he decided this form of motivation would only take them so far, and he did not want them operating out of fear or necessity.

He needed for the employees to understand why the company's survival mattered and why its mission was important enough to have brought him out of retirement. He reminded them that there were two million customers who relied on the company for their health insurance. The company needed to survive in order to provide an affordable option for these people, and to do so with an even higher level of customer care than they had previously received.

In short, the company needed to survive and thrive for the good of its customers.

Was it easy to rally the troops? No. Many employees left and found other, more stable corporate situations. But those who stayed now had a mission they could buy into: helping others by providing a valuable service. As they began to focus on helping others, it helped them, and the company, as well.

Now contrast that approach with one in which the primary goal is the *leader's* personal best interest:

- Increase departmental performance in order to be promoted.
- Win enough games to earn a raise or a job at a bigger, higher-profile school.

- Raise the stock price so that his or her options will increase in value.

None of those shortsighted goals can be the mission of a mentor leader—they simply aren't about building up other people. If the mission is all about you as the leader, you'll never get anyone to follow you for any reason other than that they have to—which will only get you so far. As a leader, you'll be rewarded when your group achieves its goals—and you should expect to be rewarded. But those rewards can't be your primary motivation. You have to derive satisfaction from seeing your group flourish and achieve its goals and to see everyone reap the benefits of that success. Remember, too, that mentor leaders are prepared to allow others to receive the credit, for the betterment of the entire organization.

✦ **Whatever your corporate mission, paint a clear and compelling picture that others can understand and embrace.**

To succeed as a mentor leader, put other people first.

Others first.

Whatever your corporate mission, paint a clear and compelling picture that others can understand and embrace.

State your mission in terms that appeal to your team's best instincts.

Persuade and empower as if you're leading and mentoring volunteers.

Others first, for maximum team performance.

ACTION STEPS

1. Put first things first. Create a culture that values people inside and outside the organization. A culture that puts the interests of others first will set a standard by which everyone in the organization will measure his or her own performance.

2. Get the culture right. The culture of an organization is the first thing other people see. It determines the direction of your organization and the way decisions are made. Get the culture right, and the rest won't necessarily be easy, but it will be easier. What can you do to start changing the culture of your organization?

3. Get everyone on the same page. How can you make your leadership more inclusive? How can you help your team to embrace the corporate mission?

4. Strengthen your organization by embracing diversity. What can you do to build on the differences within your team?

5. Break down barriers. Confident, secure leaders cross boundaries that otherwise separate society. What can you do to break down barriers inside and outside your organization?

6. Bring the best people on board. Accept candid feedback and differing opinions with the idea that someone may have a better way.

7. Accept and promote this truth for the good of the team: We are all important, but we are not indispensable.

8. Be firm in the essentials but flexible in the nonessentials. Focus on the things that really matter.

9. Treat the members of your team as you would volunteers. Mentor leaders realize the power of persuading others to follow, rather than *requiring* them to follow.

CHAPTER 8

THE METHODS OF A MENTOR LEADER: THE SEVEN E'S OF ENHANCING POTENTIAL

Blessed is the leader who seeks the best for those he serves.

AUTHOR UNKNOWN

It's time to move from theory to practical application. If I want to become a mentor leader who adds value to other people's lives and to the life of my organization, how do I get started? What do I do next? Building on our discussion of the marks and means of a mentor leader, we'll now consider some specific ways you can put mentor leadership into action.

Time to get in the game.

I hope that the book thus far has given you a greater awareness of the moments of potential impact you will have every day. I hope you've begun to appreciate the power of putting other people first and to think about becoming more intentional with the people around you. Perhaps you've already started a personal inventory of your strengths and begun to think of people you could encourage and mentor.

In this chapter, we'll look at seven key words—all beginning with the letter *E*—that describe a progression of steps that will help you mentor others while you lead them to reach their potential as team members. I'm convinced that these seven steps, along with the principles we've already discussed, will help you build an effective, high-performance organization—whether it's your business, team, church, or family.

As a mentor and a leader, I have found that I cannot move the ball forward with positive, nurturing leadership until I *engage* with those I am blessed to lead. Once I've engaged with them, I am able to *educate* and *equip*. Throughout the process, it is essential to *encourage*, *empower*, and *energize* in order to finally *elevate* the people around me.

I hope that a brief explanation of each of these steps, along with some examples, will help you get started with the mentoring opportunities right in front of you.

ENGAGE

Teamwork doesn't tolerate the inconvenience of distance.
AUTHOR UNKNOWN

Too many leaders think—mistakenly—that they must stay aloof and above the fray. They believe they should maintain a respectable distance from the people they lead so they can remain "objective" and not become entangled in the issues and concerns of their followers. I believe that's an unfortunate viewpoint that is destined to reduce the leader's potential impact and undermine the effectiveness of the team.

I believe it is critical for mentor leaders to engage with those they lead. It's impossible to mentor from a distance. Without engagement, you cannot lead effectively. You cannot mentor with empathy. You cannot inspire people to new heights and lift them to a better place in their lives. If you do not engage with those you serve, you will never understand them or know enough about them to be able to have a positive effect in their lives.

Will engagement with the people you lead make it more difficult at times to be detached and objective? Sure. But while I understand the need for objectivity in performance evaluations, for example, I've never heard "detached" and "objective" as goals for any organization. Good leadership means getting involved.

Mentor leaders walk alongside the people they lead—and they love every step. They spend time with their teams

+ **It's impossible to mentor from a distance. Without engagement, you cannot lead effectively.**

and find ways to understand each member. As a fiftysomething coach working with Generation Y or Millennial athletes, I had to find ways to plug in—whether by hiring young coaches or enlisting my teenage son's help as a "consultant." Anything that opens up the lines of communication and allows us to engage others is a step in the right direction.

One of the other ways I tried to build communication and foster engagement—and I encouraged my coaches to do this as well—was to keep an open-door policy. I rarely closed the door to my office, unless I was in a private meeting. I wanted everyone in the organization to know that they could come see me whenever they wanted. A true open-door policy is a matter of *attitude* and *approachability*, not just whether the office door is propped open. I played for a few coaches whose offices I was scared to death to enter, even when the door was standing open. I was never comfortable asking them anything or communicating beyond a surface level. On the other hand, the coaches who had the greatest positive impact on me were ones whose doors I wasn't afraid to knock on, even if they were closed.

As a leader, what kind of atmosphere have you created? Do you have an open-door policy, but no one ever comes to your office?

Whether intentionally or unintentionally, have you created an aura of detachment?

+ **A true open-door policy is a matter of *attitude* and *approachability*, not just whether the office door is propped open.**

As we've already established, mentor leaders should always be looking for ways to connect with the people they lead. One simple way to remind yourself is to keep the door to your office open as much as possible. Even though it's a passive gesture, it sends a clear signal that you are approachable. As time passes and people learn that your door truly is *open*, they will take advantage of your invitation to come in. A simple open door equals an opportunity for engagement.

Engagement is a key factor in the management style known as "management by walking around," pioneered years ago by the founders of Hewlett-Packard and popularized by Tom Peters and Bob Waterman in their 1982 best-selling book *In Search of Excellence.* This style grew from a desire to be connected. A similar idea inspires the new television show *Undercover Boss*: get the big boss involved in each aspect of the business. Based on the idea that many CEOs have become completely detached from their core business, without a clue as to what their workers do on a daily basis, the show sends corporate leaders into the trenches for some hands-on experience. As the cameras follow along, they spend a week working anonymously in various positions in their companies with the hope that they will achieve greater engagement and understanding. One such boss was actually fired from one of the positions he worked that week—spearing trash from the outer hill of a landfill. He later noted how eye-opening it was to see how hard his employees worked and how some of the executive policies he had implemented were actually making it more difficult for employees to properly perform the company's daily operations. CEOs who get connected—or reconnected—with their employees have a greater platform for implementing positive change.

Sean Payton took over as head coach of the New Orleans Saints in January 2006, only months after Hurricane Katrina had devastated the area. Although the Saints' entire 2005 home schedule had been played at sites outside of New Orleans, the team and the NFL vowed to get back to business as usual as quickly as possible to give the city something to rally around.

In order to build his coaching staff, Sean first had to sell new coaches on moving to New Orleans, which he did through his infectious enthusiasm. A number of other clubs were looking for coaches at the same time, but Sean used the challenges presented by Katrina to sell his program. He told prospective coaches that they would be part of giving hope and spirit to an entire community that needed it—and would win a lot of games in the process. He and his new staff, along with their families, stayed for months in a hotel just across the street from the airport, one of the few full-service hotels that was operational. Eventually, the coaches moved out of the hotel as they found houses, but in the meantime, they were living in the same place, sharing one another's lives—coaches, spouses, and children, learning firsthand about engagement.

I recently had an opportunity to meet with Indiana University head basketball coach Tom Crean and watch the team practice at Assembly Hall in Bloomington. Tom demonstrated his connection to his players by dressing for practice and running drills with them, as many college basketball coaches do. It reminded me of the good old days when I was young enough to do that with my players.

The older I got, the fewer routes I ran in practice and the more I had to look for other ways to engage with my players. One thing I learned to do was to allow our players to elect their own captains. I know a number of coaches who appoint captains, and I understand that approach. But I discovered with the teams I coached that even though I was engaged with my players, I wasn't always aware of who the real team leaders were, the guys who really had the respect of their teammates in the locker room. Those were the guys we wanted as our captains.

In 2009, the Colts elected four team captains. Most fans would have guessed that Peyton Manning was one of them, but they might not have figured that Gary Brackett, Adam Vinatieri, and Melvin Bullitt were the others. Though Vinatieri was a fourteen-year veteran with two Super Bowl–winning field goals to his credit, both Brackett and Bullitt had come to the Colts without much fanfare, as undrafted free agents. Still, their election as captains demonstrated that they had earned the respect of their peers. Allowing the players to vote on captains gave Gary and Melvin an opportunity to have their leadership skills recognized and rewarded.

Stay engaged. It's a sign of a great mentor leader.

EDUCATE

Good teachers help every student earn an A.
WILBUR DUNGY

I'm sure it's only natural that I believe the first step in creating leaders—after engaging with those you lead—is to educate them. After all, I was raised by two parents who were teachers, and I learned to coach in the Paul Brown school of football. Brown, the legendary coach of the Cleveland Browns and Cincinnati Bengals, was known for making extensive use of classroom work and teaching. Chuck Noll played for Coach Brown in Cleveland and later adopted many of his coaching ideas when he became the head coach in Pittsburgh, where I got my start in coaching.

Education is an essential building block of mentor leadership. Workers who are new to a task cannot be empowered and elevated until they've been educated in what to do. First things first.

Because mentor leadership is all about helping others become the best they can be, it is built on a foundation of teaching, helping, and guiding. Our goal should be to help everyone earn an A—or whatever the equivalent measure of success is in our organizations. Mentor leaders must not be content to merely teach the group from the front of the room; they must take a hands-on, one-on-one approach to mentoring individual lives. By providing others with opportunities to grow, we help them become even more valuable members of the team, even as we're building the overall strength of the team.

✛ **Mentor leaders must take a hands-on, one-on-one approach to mentoring individual lives.**

Dave Driscoll, my high school football coach, was a team builder and a teacher. At the time, though, like many teenagers would, I felt he was too strict and controlling with the team. I chafed a little under his guidance in high school. Ironically, though I believed he was controlling when I played for him, he told me later that he had given me more latitude than anyone else he had ever coached. And though we were looking at things from entirely different perspectives, I think we both may have been partially correct. I wanted more freedom in my ability to lead, but he understood, wisely, that there were some things I wasn't ready to handle. His job was to educate me in those areas, and as I learned, I would get more autonomy. As I look back on it now, Coach Driscoll was a lot more patient and a much better teacher than I gave him credit for when I was sixteen.

I saw the importance of education from a different perspective when I retired from coaching and started broadcasting. In 2009, former New England Patriot strong safety Rodney Harrison and I joined the cast of NBC's *Football Night in America*. Being totally new to television, we were in need of plenty of education—me, especially.

I knew that Dick Ebersol was the chairman of NBC Sports, and I already knew the on-air talent; but I had no idea who the other players were—including Sam Flood, who I soon learned is the producer of the show.

Poor Sam had been dealt a bad hand. Here he was, a veteran producer who had brought together broadcasts of the Olympics, the Kentucky Derby, and the Stanley Cup Finals, and who had just lost two Emmy-winning broadcasters, Cris Collinsworth and Bob Costas, to be at the game site each week, to be replaced in-studio by two broadcast rookies: Rodney and me. I'm sure that breaking in a new crew wasn't a dream come true for Sam, but he worked hard to help us improve and to build us into a functioning unit.

To learn about us, Sam took us out to dinner and the three of us played a few rounds of golf with Dan Patrick—which was more fun for Rodney and Sam than for Dan and me, I'm afraid. In the process, Sam began to understand our personalities. He was evaluating our strengths as he trained us.

Sam knows sports broadcasting inside and out, and thankfully he was very patient with us. But what I appreciated most was how he put us in positions to use our strengths. Rodney is a strong personality, very smart and spontaneous. I am more analytical and not nearly as funny—on purpose, anyway. To get us started, Sam let Rodney react to *how* teams played, while I might break down *why* a play worked. As we got more comfortable and got better at other parts of the job, our roles gradually expanded.

By the end of the season, we had meshed with the veteran broadcasters into a pretty fair team. If nothing else, Rodney and I at least knew how to put our earpieces in—which was progress.

Along the way, Sam took a personal interest in me and produced some feature pieces that I wanted to do—such as one on singer Michael W. Smith and another on a Tampa-area high school that was implementing the Uncommon program—with a focus on making them great, simply because they were important to me.

Through it all, Sam taught us and put each of us in a position to do what we did best, without any concern for whether he received credit—which is exactly what a leader is supposed to do.

In football, as in other areas of life, you can't take the basic skills for granted. John Bonamego, the special teams coordinator for the Miami Dolphins, points out that he can't assume that his players know the proper techniques for playing special teams, even though they have reached the NFL. For instance, he has to make sure that defensive players know how to block when they find themselves on the punt return or kickoff return teams, and he has to teach tackling to the receivers and other offensive players who play on the punt and kickoff coverage teams. Some players know the basics but may not have practiced them. Others may not have those skills at all. It all starts with education.

Chan Gailey has twice been named a head coach in the NFL, and he has served as offensive coordinator for several other teams. But one of his most fascinating coaching ideas was one he implemented a few years ago as head coach at Georgia Tech: He required his freshman players to take a leadership course from him for thirty minutes a week during their first semester. This was in addition to their regular classroom course load—which at Tech is no small matter—and their football meetings and practices. He believed that those players would eventually be leading his team, "and after that, our country." Wanting them to start thinking about what it means to be a leader, he made sure that his leadership course was an integral part of their Georgia Tech education. Chan wanted to ensure, from the earliest moment possible, that he was helping to train the next generation of leaders—for their own benefit, for the benefit of the team and the school, as well as for the nation.

A real mentor leader.

When I hear the word *educate,* I think of how Chuck Noll would approach me after a bad play. Even though my mistake may have been costly, Chuck was usually calm.

Ever the teacher.

Ever the engager.

Ever the mentor leader.

EQUIP

Our job as a coaching staff is to show you what to do and how to do it. Your job as players is to do it consistently.
CHUCK NOLL

Mentor leaders create an environment in which others can be productive and excel. They set the parameters and guidelines for the task, project and continually recast the vision, and then provide the tools and equipment needed for everyone to be successful in their assignment and to ultimately accomplish their mission. In essence, they strive to furnish what is needed for the task—physically, mentally, emotionally, and spiritually—and to accomplish the mission.

I think, for most people, poorly defined tasks are one of the highest areas of dissatisfaction. How often have you been given an assignment without being told how to do it or what's expected? Are you expected to bring back a recommendation or a report? In writing? Or maybe you were supposed to produce a signed contract. Who knows?

+ For most people, poorly defined tasks are one of the highest areas of dissatisfaction.

But even if we've been properly educated and informed, we may not have the proper tools. Equipping goes hand in hand with educating if we want people to perform to their highest potential.

And just because we've gone through the process once doesn't mean we won't have to do it again. Picture a young coach I've hired as my defensive quality-control coach. He will work under the defensive coordinator, providing him with breakdowns of opponents' videos and drawing up play cards of other teams' offenses to allow the scout team to simulate those plays in practice. That's the job description in a nutshell, but what exactly does the defensive coordinator want? Many young coaches have to rewrite their reports several times because they didn't know what the coordinator really wanted.

"Why did you include those plays in the report? Their quarterback was hurt in that game. They'll run an entirely different offense against us when he is back in the lineup."

"Why didn't you note that the other team blitzed when they ran this play? The quarterback changed the play at the line."

These are things the coordinator knows when he watches the tapes, and he assumes the young assistant should know them as well. But the newcomer doesn't because it has never been explained to him. Once the coordinator lays it out and shows the other coach what he wants, the young coach can deliver what the coordinator needs. Mentor leaders understand that educating and equipping with the necessary information and expectations to accomplish the task must go hand in hand.

All of life is a learning process. We may be empowered and elevated in certain areas while we're being educated and equipped in others.

Jim Zorn says that his father would often try his hand at tasks around the house and then call in a professional if needed. Jim grew up with a respect for having the right tool for the job. He views equipping players to perform to the best of their ability as providing a "tool bag" to the players he coaches.

> ✛ **Mentor leaders understand that educating and equipping must go hand in hand.**

When Jim was the quarterbacks coach in Seattle, the Seahawks acquired Matt Hasselbeck from Green Bay. Despite his limited experience at the time, Matt was slated to be the starting quarterback. Jim's job was to prepare him as quickly as possible to play. He started

Matt's development step by step—progressing from the simpler elements of quarterbacking to the more complex. As they gradually added items to Matt's tool bag, they were able to put him in more situations where he could make decisions that would directly affect the outcome of the play.

Jim said they put in the heaviest work on tool development in the off-season, adding incrementally to Matt's repertoire as he mastered each successive skill. They didn't throw everything at him at once and hope that it would all stick. In the early years, they worked repeatedly on certain drills: footwork; release; pump, reload, and throw. The combination of several years of work and Matt's natural talent finally resulted in his being named to the Pro Bowl three times. Jim said that, during those Pro Bowl years, film sessions became a game between Matt and him. They would try to identify moments in the games that came straight from the drills: "Look at my feet—that's the drill we did last summer."

Equipping is an ongoing process for a mentor leader. As various tools are mastered, we can keep honing them and looking to add more.

Coach Noll understood the importance of equipping players with a *mind-set* as well as with the tools they needed for the task ahead. When the Steelers first went to the Super Bowl, in 1975 against the Minnesota Vikings, I was still a student at the University of Minnesota. But from all the time I spent in Pittsburgh later on, it still feels like "us" when I think about that game. The Vikings were more experienced, having been to the Super Bowl twice before, and they had an excellent defense predicated on stopping the run—which they had done all year behind Carl Eller and Alan Page.

✛ **Coach Noll understood the importance of equipping players with a *mind-set* as well as with the tools they needed for the task ahead.**

We were a running team, and the pundits were all trying to guess what would happen if the Vikings stopped our running game. How would we adjust? When Chuck Noll was asked that question in a pre-game press conference, his response reminded me of something my dad would say: "Leaving the game plan is a sign of panic, and panic is not in our game plan."

Chuck's message was clear: We won't adjust; we won't adapt. We will do what we do best and make the Vikings adjust.

The players told me later that the game was won at that point. The Steelers, in fact, never trailed—taking a 2–0 lead into halftime and eventually winning 16–6.

Coach Noll had equipped his players mentally and physically to get the job done. He did the same thing so many times with the teams I was a part of that I began to see it as one of his greatest strengths. He believed in his staff and his game plans.

Of course, there could have been a downside to his strategy—he could have been wrong. As Chuck told me when I started coaching, stubbornness is only a virtue if you're right. When you're wrong, it's just another character flaw. His genius was in knowing when he was right.

ENCOURAGE

Correction does much, but encouragement does more.
GOETHE

Encouragement is the fuel that powers our efforts to engage, educate, and equip. Nothing does more to lubricate the rough spots than a good dose of encouragement.

> Nothing does more to lubricate the rough spots than a good dose of encouragement.

Mentor leaders care. Mentor leaders lift others up. Mentor leaders encourage.

Not everyone is good at encouragement—I understand that. And now that I've acknowledged it, you may never use it as an excuse again. If you have been called to lead—and every one of us has that calling in some aspect of our lives—then you have been called to encourage. Mentor leaders are encouragers—period. I realize that I emphasized earlier the importance of playing to your strengths and finding others to complement your weaknesses, but

+ It's not just in tough situations that people need encouragement.

encouragement is one aspect of leadership that you can't delegate—you simply have to master it, whether you are predisposed to it or not.

You can't use the culture you were raised in as an excuse either. Please don't say, "Well, we just kept to ourselves when I was growing up. We didn't smile much and didn't show our emotions." Or, "I never got much encouragement as a kid, so it's hard for me to do it now." You can turn those perceived deficiencies from the past into motivation to make a difference today. Why perpetuate a culture without encouragement?

Certainly Christians should be joyful and encouraging, because Jesus was an encourager across every sociological barrier He encountered. Mentor leaders must learn to encourage others.

And it's not just in tough situations that people need encouragement. Even when things are going smoothly, it's important to build people up. When I started coaching at Tampa Bay, we were not winning, and therefore we received our share of criticism from fans and the media. During my first year, I was careful in my postgame evaluations with our players to point out the good things they were doing and the progress we were making as a team, even though we weren't winning consistently. Once we started winning and the media coverage became more positive, I talked less and less about what we were doing well and more about the corrections we needed to make going forward to improve. Without realizing it, I lost the encouraging tone with my team. Finally, after I had reviewed a game during a long *winning* streak, one of our veteran players asked me, "Will we ever play a game where you're satisfied?" I was extremely satisfied with how they were playing. The only problem was they didn't know it. It was a lesson I tried to remember from then on. Everyone needs encouragement, even when things are going well.

Not every situation calls for encouragement. Sometimes direction, correction, or admonishment is the most appropriate response. If you're a parent of young children, as I am, you should be able to get an instant mental snapshot of these situations. You may not buy the premise that encouragement is *always* needed, as I believe, but let me ask you this: Who really benefits from *dis*couragement? More often than not, encouragement is exactly what is needed. As a mentor leader, you're probably better off *over*using encouragement than *under*using it.

✢ **You're probably better off *over*using encouragement than *under*using it.**

Billy Donovan, the head basketball coach at the University of Florida, has made a football-crazy school stop and take notice of its basketball team. With a career winning percentage over .700, Billy has taken the Gators to nine NCAA Tournament berths and has won the national championship twice.

Billy will tell you that one of the most important things he does in molding young kids into tomorrow's leaders is to encourage them. He does this hands-on, on a daily basis, at practice and in games. He encourages his players by the way he talks to the media, trying to soften criticism that may come their way while using his own comments to build them up. He also brings in outside speakers to supplement his constant infusion of encouragement.

Through these outside speakers—everyone from sports leaders to military leaders to business leaders—Billy pursues a dual purpose: He looks to educate his players on a variety of skills while at the same time reminding them that they can be people of great achievement, both on and off the court.

I learned the importance of firsthand encouragement during my second year as the Buccaneers' head coach. I had come out of the

Steelers tradition of "Next Man Up," which was Chuck Noll's way of making sure that every player was ready to go if the player in front of him got hurt. Next Man Up was another expression of Chuck's belief that individual players were important but not indispensable. If a starter was going to miss a game, Chuck didn't spend time lamenting the fact; he simply adapted the game plan to make use of the new starter's strengths and pressed on, confident that the Steeler Way would carry us through.

Obviously, the next man up wouldn't be as proficient—otherwise he'd be the starter. But we also didn't need him to do anything extraordinary—just do his job to the best of his ability. Some of the other guys might have to step up and do a little more, but as a team we'd be fine. Coach Noll made sure that we all knew that every day. It was simply part of the fabric of the Steelers.

I wanted to weave the same mind-set into our system in Tampa Bay, and in the fourth game of the season, we had the perfect opportunity. We had opened the season with three straight wins, but in the third game—a road win over Minnesota—Warren Sapp, our star defensive tackle, was injured. He suffered a broken bone in his hand that had our doctors frantically trying to construct a soft cast that would allow him to play. They weren't sure they could, and I didn't want the entire week of preparation for our fourth game to be consumed by a "will he play or won't he?" dialogue. Warren was becoming a dominant force for us, and he was one of our defensive leaders. For that reason, I wanted the players to fully appreciate the concept of Next Man Up—so I ruled Warren out right away, without even giving him a voice in the decision. We simply moved on to his replacement and moved ahead with our game plan. We had another starter on defense, linebacker Rufus Porter, who was also injured. So my message to our young team was, "Don't worry about who's *not* playing. We will win this game with the guys who are healthy." I didn't want our young team thinking about the guys we *didn't* have.

The next Sunday, we had our first sold-out stadium in years, and we beat the Miami Dolphins, 31–21. Leadership mission accomplished. The guys had bought into Next Man Up and saw that it worked.

Congratulations to me.

And then Warren Sapp, the forgotten man in all of this, walked up to me. "You never asked me if I could play this week," he said. "You just acted as if I didn't exist. I thought you wanted me as one of the leaders of this defense, and I was just an afterthought."

I had to take a step back from the moment of reveling in the win and recognize that I hadn't handled the situation properly with Warren. I explained that I wasn't ignoring him but that I was trying to send a message to the team by the way I handled his injury situation. I felt that ruling him out early in the week would be the best thing for the rest of our players' confidence. I didn't want the team thinking all week that he might play and then finding out right before the game that he couldn't go. That would have been deflating. And I didn't want them to be distracted by something they couldn't control—the condition of Warren's hand.

Once I explained it, he understood, but I learned an important lesson that day. I needed to communicate better because even a person as self-confident and talented as Warren Sapp needed affirmation and encouragement.

A good lesson for a young coach and a budding mentor leader.

Did I mention that a mentor leader is an encourager? Period.

EMPOWER

As we look ahead . . . leaders will be those who empower others.
BILL GATES

Once the people you lead are ready, it's time to turn them loose. But not before they're ready. As a mentor leader, you have a responsibility to engage, educate, equip, and encourage them first—and at every appropriate point thereafter, as well. You can't just walk in and empower them. If they're not ready, you're only setting them up to fail.

The way Lofton Greene coached his River Rouge High School basketball team was a good example of thorough preparation and "not talking during the test." He made sure his teams were so well prepared that he didn't have to constantly direct them *while* they were playing. As their coach, he was still accountable for their well-being, of course. In times of crisis or during time-outs, he was there to offer encouragement and guidance, but he had taught them his system and prepared them so well for their opponent that when the game started, he trusted that the players would be able to execute on their own. He would sit calmly and watch them "take the test," and they usually got a very good grade.

That is true empowerment: preparation followed by appropriate freedom.

The University of Miami football teams of the 1980s and '90s were great examples of empowerment. Starting with coach Howard Schnellenberger and then continuing under Jimmy Johnson and Dennis Erickson, those teams had clear and challenging expectations placed on them. Practices were tough, the competition for playing time was intense, and the commitment to winning was second to none. Not only were they very talented football teams, they were also a football family that was extremely committed to one another.

> ✦ **That is true empowerment: preparation followed by appropriate freedom.**

The coaches laid out what it would take to have a highly successful college football program, and then they turned it over to the players to perform. By the time Warren Sapp came through the program in the early 1990s, the entire preparation process was well established. The players totally believed in the system, and it was self-policing. As

Warren described it, if he wasn't focused on the practice field or in the weight room as a freshman, an upperclassman was there to rectify the problem. The older players took it upon themselves to educate and equip him until they could trust that he wouldn't let the team down. The coaches didn't even have to get involved. By the time Warren reached his sophomore and junior seasons, he understood what was expected and was able to hold the next group accountable as well.

It's no accident they had such success at Miami. They had a squad full of leaders—leaders the coaches had prepared and empowered to fulfill their mission.

Coach Noll's system was much the same. He set the course and gave us the guidelines, but often allowed the veteran players to lead the way. They believed in his methods, and they made sure Coach's directives were followed. In the process, we developed accountability through player leadership, which dispersed itself throughout the ranks. The coaches—mentor leaders led themselves by their head coach—empowered the veterans to carry on the mission.

Dwight White, the great Steelers defensive lineman, played in all four of the Steelers' Super Bowl wins of the 1970s. He almost missed the first one against the Vikings, however, as he was hospitalized all week with pneumonia, complicated by pleurisy. He lost eighteen pounds that week but still emerged to play in the game on a cold, slippery turf field in New Orleans. Coach Noll was prepared to play without Dwight, but Dwight wouldn't hear of it. In fact, he scored Pittsburgh's first points in a Super Bowl by sacking Fran Tarkenton for a safety and the 2–0 halftime lead that the Steelers would never relinquish.

And then he went back into the hospital after the game. I don't know how Dwight was able to play that day, but it was typical of the attitude that Coach Noll had instilled in us by empowering the players. No one wanted to let the team down.

When Jim Zorn was head coach of the Washington Redskins, his offensive coordinator was his good friend Sherman Smith. Jim empowered Sherm in a number of areas, including accountability. I know from experience that there aren't many assistant coaches willing to be honest in evaluating the *head coach's* performance, but Jim knew that Sherm would give him honest feedback, and he wanted Sherm's input on how he was doing and where he needed to make adjustments.

In Jim's first season as head coach of the Redskins, they won six of their first eight games and were 7–4 by the time the New York Giants came to town. In that game, as Jim tells it, everything that could have gone wrong did, and his emotions got the best of him. Jim began barking at everyone—coaches on the headset, players, even the ball boy. At one point, the ball boy—who is not actually a boy but a grown man—was prepared to throw a wet ball into the game. Jim shouted at him, took the ball, and threw it into the stands. In mid-game.

The next day, Sherm walked into Jim's office, closed the door, and read Jim the riot act. Sherm knew of Jim's "act medium" mantra, and he told him he hadn't lived up to it. He hadn't maximized his own performance, and by his behavior he had hurt his team's chances to win the game. Jim had been totally unavailable to those who were counting on him; in fact, Sherm had taken his headset off on three separate occasions because of Jim's barking.

Because he had empowered Sherman Smith to speak into his life, Jim received some important feedback. He took it to heart and made the appropriate corrections, staying under control from that point forward.

Another example of how to empower an organization is being shown by Charlie Strong, a friend of mine and the new head football coach of the University of Louisville. As the new leader of a program that hasn't seen much success lately, Charlie is trying to change the culture and get the team back on a winning track. To do so, he wants to educate and then empower his players. In much the same way that coach Howard Schnellenberger and his successors at the University of Miami did when they rebuilt their program, Charlie is trying to instill a specific culture by including his veteran players and establishing veteran leadership.

For his first spring practices at Louisville, Charlie split the squad into eight groups, each led by a senior he had selected based on a combination of game experience and academic record. Each of those eight groups is comprised of an intentional mixture of players—linemen, skill players, and so forth—and they competed over several weeks in a variety of challenges, ranging from football workouts to classroom achievement. Charlie allowed the group leaders to oversee discipline and motivation, looking to instill ownership and self-control over the squad, step by step.

Empowerment. At some point, a mentor leader must turn others loose to do their jobs.

ENERGIZE

Without inspiration, the best powers of the mind are dormant.
There is a tinder in us which needs to be quickened with sparks.
JOHANN GOTTFRIED VON HERDER

Great leaders energize and inspire those they lead. Even as they face their own daily struggles and stresses, mentor leaders look for ways to energize and motivate the people around them.

The story is told of Major General Matthew Ridgway during World War II, who parachuted in with his men behind the beach landing at Normandy. At one point, during fierce fighting to take a criti-

✛ **Great leaders energize and inspire those they lead.**

cal bridge, the men under his command saw Ridgway standing at the point of heaviest fire. He was in there with his troops, inspiring them, energizing them to continue on no matter what they faced.

John Bonamego points out that special teams coaches are among the only assistant coaches in the NFL who have to be a little creative in finding ways to energize their players—because many of those players would rather not be playing on special teams. Special teams do the dirty work in the NFL—a role that is absolutely necessary to success but not at all glamorous. A third-string linebacker, for example, is more eager to do defensive drills so he can become a starting linebacker than he is to do special teams drills. The special teams coach not only has to educate his players on the importance of special teams, but through that process, he must also inspire them to play with the passion that special teams requires.

Perry Fewell took over the head coaching reins of the Buffalo Bills in the middle of the 2009 season. That's always a tough situation. The ship has sailed, but it's sinking. That's why you got the job. And now you have to get the ship headed in the right direction without the benefit of time for planning and preparation that a preseason provides. You have only a few days to reorient your staff and players and get ready for the next game.

Perry said that one of his most important tasks was to get the players to a point of believing in themselves—and quickly. He began preaching the benefits of viewing themselves more as a group than as a collection of individuals. "Powerful Beyond Measure" became his rallying cry. The concept was that together they were more powerful than the measurement of their individual talents.

In one particular game, he showed that a little faith can go a long way toward energizing an organization. The Bills were tied with Miami, 14–14, with just over three minutes to play in the game. Facing a fourth down from Miami's 39-yard line, Perry had a decision to make. A field goal would give his team the lead; but at that distance, an attempt was risky. The safe play would have been to punt, play defense, and hope to get the ball back with a chance to score. However, he had been telling his players, "Don't be afraid to win." They had played tentatively all year, as if they were waiting for something bad to happen in every game. Not surprisingly, it often had. Funny how those self-fulfilling prophecies have a way of coming true.

Perry knew that the spot of the ball was at the outer limit of his field goal kicker's range, but he called him over and said, "Rian, I believe you can make this. Do you agree?" Rian Lindell, the Bills' kicker, nodded, and Perry sent him out for the field goal attempt. Everyone knew what was on the line. If Lindell missed, the Dolphins would have the ball near midfield late in a tie game.

Instead, Lindell split the uprights with plenty of distance to spare. The players on the sideline were ecstatic; the energy level was off the charts. All from a little faith.

The Bills took the field needing to keep their lead. But instead of playing not to lose, Perry told them to win with authority and not to wait for something to happen. Again they responded—with two interceptions, both followed by a touchdown. Final score: Buffalo 31, Miami 14.

A game in the balance became a decisive victory, all from a coach's decision to believe in his kicker. A single spark had set the team ablaze.

Energize. Inspire. Motivate.

The mentor leader does this—intentionally.

ELEVATE

Teamwork: Simply stated, it is less me and more we.
AUTHOR UNKNOWN

What are the goals in place for your organization? To build the best team possible? To win the most games? To develop the top-rated sales force, one that makes its quota every quarter? To have the highest graduation rate of any high school in the state? Those are all worthy goals, and as a leader you have to function with the goals of your organization in mind. But the ultimate goal of every mentor leader is to build other leaders. The regenerative idea that leaders produce leaders, who in turn produce leaders—is a powerful concept for mentor leaders and their organizations. At the heart of this regeneration is the principle of *elevation*—raising people up.

Many leaders struggle with this essential concept. Elevating is difficult. It seems paradoxical to elevate someone who might end up taking your place. But raising up leaders is the truly selfless goal of every mentor leader, the culmination of focusing on others. To elevate your followers means to help them reach their God-given potential, even if it means preparing them to replace *you*. It may also mean that you prepare them to leave your organization for better opportunities elsewhere—perhaps even with your competitors.

When I arrived in Tampa Bay as the new head coach, I knew that one coach I wanted to hire as an assistant was Herm Edwards. As I mentioned before, I knew that Herm's strengths complemented my own and also offset some of my weaknesses. I felt he would be a tremendous help to me and the Buccaneers. But I also felt that we could help him achieve his own goals. Herm had started his career in coaching, but at the time he was working in the personnel department for the Kansas City Chiefs. I'm sure he would have done well on the administrative side of the game, but I knew his heart was in coaching. He was a great teacher, with the skills to eventually become a head coach himself, and I thought we had the perfect environment in Tampa for him to develop those skills.

> ✢ Raising up leaders is the truly selfless goal of every mentor leader, the culmination of focusing on others.

To that end, I hired him as assistant head coach, and in the same way that Denny Green had elevated me in Minnesota, I tried to create opportunities for Herm to be involved in every aspect of my job.

In his role, he helped me with discipline and scheduling and learned some of the issues that head coaches confront.

The whole time Herm was with me in Tampa, the clock was ticking. We both knew he would be leaving someday. And though I didn't look forward to losing him, I knew he was too good not to get snapped up by some other team. I also felt it was part of my job to help all my assistants develop and move on. Herm had several opportunities to leave and become a defensive coordinator, but he wasn't interested in that. His goal was to be a head coach, and he was patient enough to stay with us until that happened.

Sure enough, in January 2001, Herm was hired as head coach of the New York Jets. I lost him through elevating him. As much as it hurt me to see him go, and as much as it hurt the organization to lose a great coach, I was happy and excited for Herm. It was what we both had hoped for when he came to work for me.

Several more coaches eventually left my staff to make their mark elsewhere as leaders, and I am proud of each one of them. Perhaps the result I'm most proud of, though, is the elevation of Jim Caldwell. Jim didn't have to go to another team to make his mark; he ended up replacing *me* in Indianapolis.

Jim Caldwell is an extremely bright and fine football coach. When I hired him from Wake Forest in 2001 to coach our quarterbacks in Tampa, almost immediately I could see a quiet, determined confidence that allowed him to lead without being overbearing. That was precisely the style of leadership I was trying to foster.

In 2005, I began to contemplate retirement at the close of each season. At the same time, Jim, who had come with me to the Colts and was still our quarterbacks coach, was drawing interest from other clubs to become their head coach. Jim Irsay decided that he wanted to keep Jim in Indianapolis to become the head coach of the Colts whenever I finally decided to retire from football—a decision with which I completely agreed.

Toward that end, we elevated Jim's position to that of assistant head coach, and I became more intentional about preparing Jim for the day when he would take over. He didn't need me to educate or equip him, because he had developed his own tool bag during his long coaching career. What he needed, however, was for me to empower him with others and allow him to engage with more than just the quarterbacks under his direct line of responsibility. We began to create opportunities for Jim to be included in the decision-making process on personnel; to interact with the defense and special teams; and to be prepared so that the transition to head coach, whenever it occurred, would be seamless. He would make his own decisions at that point—as he ultimately did when he took over—but those decisions would be based on a complete grasp of the situation.

Jim took over the Colts in 2009. As the season wore on and the Colts were still unbeaten under Jim's leadership, Nathan joked that I was fast becoming "Tony who?" in the city of Indianapolis. He was kidding—I think—but not far off base. But that was fine with me. I was happy to see the Colts winning and Jim doing so well in his first year as head coach. As a mentor leader, the success of the people you've elevated is what you like to see. It's not about getting the credit; it's about helping the organization, and everyone in it, be the best they can be. If you've been building leaders all around you, then the organization certainly shouldn't fall apart when you leave. An organization that remains totally dependent on a particular personality seems to me one that has not been properly led. If leaders are focused on multiplying their efforts and growing other leaders for long-term, sustainable success, they will succeed in building organizations that are full of leaders—and eventually replace themselves.

+ It's not about getting the credit; it's about helping the organization, and everyone in it, be the best they can be.

Some leaders don't want to be replaced. They think it reflects better on their leadership abilities if the organization simply can't run without them, and thus they are tempted to leave others in the dark.

I'll say it again: That is a sign of poor leadership. I always wanted the teams I coached to be in better shape when I left than when I got there. I also wanted the organization to continue to thrive after I was gone. That's how I saw my job as a mentor leader.

Engage, educate, equip, encourage, empower, energize, and elevate.

Those are the methods for maximizing the potential of any individual, team, organization, or institution for ultimate success and significance.

Those are the methods of a mentor leader.

ACTION STEPS

1. Be engaged with those you lead in order for them to trust that you care and want to believe in you. Leadership is a "contact" sport.

2. Help every team member earn an A. Educate them for success.

3. Equip those you lead. Create an environment and provide the resources and the proper tools—physical, mental, spiritual, and emotional—for the team to be successful.

4. Take every opportunity to encourage the people you lead. When in doubt, do it. Then do it again.

5. Once your team is ready, stop teaching and let them "take the test." Empower them by letting them go.

6. Energize your team's efforts by believing in them. The energy to go forward and the inspiration to achieve will come from you.

7. Develop your team members as leaders. The mentor leader's ultimate goal is to build leaders who will leave to lead elsewhere, or who will be elevated to fill the mentor leader's role.

CHAPTER 9

THE MEASURE OF A MENTOR LEADER: BUILDING OTHER LIVES OF IMPACT

The first question that the priest asked, the first question that the Levite asked was: "If I stop to help this man, what will happen to me?" But . . . the good Samaritan . . . reversed the question: "If I do not stop to help this man, what will happen to him?"
MARTIN LUTHER KING JR.

So what is the point of all this? If we lead with character, courage, and competence; if we cast a compelling vision and inspire people to work passionately to achieve a common mission; if we model the message and recognize the moments when we can make a difference; if we educate, equip, and elevate the people around us, what does it all add up to? What does it all mean?

Very simply, the mentor leader adds value to the lives of others, to make the lives of other people better.

If leadership isn't about us and what we can get for ourselves, which I have suggested it should not be, then the fleeting treasures by which so many people gauge their worth—the promotions, raises, accolades, and awards—are no longer measuring sticks. Instead, the success of a mentor leader can be measured with things of signifi-cance: lives of impact, lives that are better because of your leadership.

✦ **Start right where you are, with the people right around you, doing something as simple as engaging with them and talking.**

We've shared a lot in these pages. Maybe you're thinking, *That's a lot to remember.* Don't worry about remembering it. Think instead about beginning to live what we've talked about—each and every day, in every setting of your life.

And let me encourage you to start right where you are, with the people right around you, doing something as simple as engaging with them and talking. Sometimes the smallest things we do have the biggest impact.

Just start.

THE JOURNEY: ADDING VALUE EVERY MOMENT

The true meaning of life is to plant trees, under whose shade you do not expect to sit.

NELSON HENDERSON

At the end of the day, the journey is about adding value to others' lives, which ultimately will impact your organization for good.

Jim Brewer was an All-American basketball player at the University of Minnesota who also played on the 1972 U.S. Olympic basketball team. He was an amazingly gifted player and the driving force behind Minnesota's rise from Big-Ten doormat to conference champion. When I arrived on the campus for my freshman year, in the summer of 1973, Jim had just been drafted as the second overall pick in the NBA by the Cleveland Cavaliers. He was truly a big man on campus, and I was a scrawny freshman, but for some reason, just before he left campus to join the Cavaliers, Jim took the time to sit down with me to talk about a few things he felt he needed to share.

It was probably a fifteen-minute conversation that took place more than three decades ago, but my memory of it is still vivid, and the impact of Jim's words has stayed with me my entire adult life. I had been raised by two lifelong teachers who had always preached the value of an education, but now I was on my own and would make my own decisions—decisions that would affect my future more than I understood at the time. And like most freshman student-athletes, my focus when I arrived on campus was much more on *athlete* than *student*.

Jim told me that he had earned his degree, despite missing classroom time to participate in the Olympics, not to mention the time spent under the demanding rigors of four years of basketball. He told me that I shouldn't leave college owing anything to anyone. I assumed he was referring to taking money from boosters or alumni—and he was—but it was also more than that.

He told me not to take anything extra, either from the university or from anyone else. He said that I needed to be able to leave with a clean slate, as he was. When the time came, I needed to be able to leave college without having to look back and feel tied to any obligations incurred during my time there. He had seen others start out in life after college feeling as if they owed something to someone.

I nodded my understanding, but then he looked me straight in the eye and said, "Not owing *anyone* includes yourself, Tony." I was surprised and a little confused about what he meant.

Jim continued, saying that I had an opportunity to use college sports to get my degree, to set myself up for the future, and to make friends and build relationships—and I should do all those things, starting with earning my degree. "If you don't leave here with your degree," he said, "you will have cheated yourself, and you'll leave here owing yourself something. Don't let that happen."

It all made sense, and it stuck with me throughout my time at the university. I followed Jim's advice, and because of it I have friends and solid relationships that have stood the test of time and distance. I left owing nothing to anyone, and I left with my degree in hand.

I didn't realize it at the time, but Jim had mentored me through that special situation. We didn't have a relationship developed over time, but he used the opportunity he had—in a few minutes on his way to the NBA—to have an important and lasting impact on my life.

Some mentoring relationships last for years and result in deep friendships. Others can happen in a moment of sharing the wisdom of your experience with someone standing right before you. The key is to look for opportunities and be ready to act.

In that special moment, Jim Brewer added value to my life.

Richard Farmer was the first pastor Lauren and I had after we were married. Although I was attending church to learn about my spiritual life, over time it became apparent that what Pastor Farmer was teaching applied to both my coaching and my family life as well. As a young coach and husband, I gleaned important insights from what he shared each week and at other times we were together. Whether Pastor Farmer consciously viewed it this way or not, he was mentoring me in both those areas of my life.

I remember in particular one Easter Sunday. Lauren and I arrived at the early service to find a man in the balcony dressed in a white robe and playing "Christ the Lord Is Risen Today" on the trumpet. It was incredibly moving—so much so that I made a point to call Pastor Farmer to thank him for including the trumpet solo as part of the service.

He really appreciated my encouragement because it seems he was getting a lot of calls from people who didn't like that part of the service.

"Because of the trumpet?" I asked. I figured I had misunderstood.

"Because of the trumpet," he said. Apparently, some people in our congregation had felt that the trumpet performance wasn't appropriate for a worship service. Having instruments in church wasn't right. Plus, he was told, "We've never done it this way before."

I'm sure he was a little hurt because he felt he had done something that would edify his fellow worshipers; but he explained to me that when you're the leader, not everyone will be happy with your decisions.

I realized at that point that his struggles in the church were no different from some of my issues on the football field, and I turned to him more and more to mentor me in my application of the Bible to my everyday life and work.

By mentoring me, Pastor Farmer was simply adding value to another person's life.

I've seen examples of adding value time and again since then, most recently by my broadcasting friend James Brown. In 2009, he and I stayed at the same New York hotel as we fulfilled our weekend broadcasting duties. Early in the season, JB called to invite me to a Bible study he was hosting. When I arrived at his room, I found him surrounded by members of the hotel staff—a bellman and people from maintenance and food services.

+ **When you're the leader, not everyone will be happy with your decisions.**

JB explained that he had become friends with these people over the last year, talking in passing about things that mattered to each of them. Eventually, they decided to get together more formally when JB was in town to broadcast, and they began a Bible study.

It didn't matter to JB that he wasn't in a direct position of leadership. What mattered was that he could build into other people's lives, one on one.

And in the process, they could build into his life as well.

SHARING THE JOURNEY

John's disciples came to him and said, "Rabbi, the man you met on the other side of the Jordan River, the one you identified as the Messiah, is also baptizing people. And everybody is going to him instead of coming to us."

John replied, "No one can receive anything unless God gives it from heaven. You yourselves know how plainly I told you, 'I am not the Messiah. I am only here to prepare the way for him.' It's the bridegroom who marries the bride, and the best man is simply glad to stand with him and hear his vows. Therefore, I am filled with joy at his success. He must become greater and greater, and I must become less and less."

JOHN 3:26-30

Handing off: John the Baptist

You've heard it enough by now: It's not about you. It's not about me. It's about others. Embracing that truth is no more important than when, as a mentor leader, you recognize the need to enlist the help of someone else to further add value to the life of another.

I love the leadership story of John the Baptist. Here was a guy with a great number of followers, who was baptizing many and preaching a message of repentance and turning to God. He clearly was making an impact and had quite a following—pretty heady stuff.

At the same time, he never lost sight of his mission: preparing the way for Jesus Christ, who was to come after him. John was very clear about his role in all that was unfolding in and around

Galilee and Judea. Eventually John urged his own disciples to go and follow Jesus.

I'm sure that wasn't an easy thing for John to do. Power, control, and fame can all be enticing. But releasing those around us to other leaders who might serve them better is one of the things we have to evaluate. If mentor leadership is about adding value to the lives of others, about making them better, shouldn't we always evaluate what is best for them and when necessary help them to find better opportunities?

John's example is a great model for us, but it's definitely hard to put into practice. I don't want to lose a good young coach because he feels he can learn more from someone coaching another team. And it's not human nature to admit that someone in whom we've invested a lot of time and energy really might learn more from someone else. But if we care about the other person, we have to be willing to acknowledge that, just as John the Baptist did with his disciples.

> ✛ Releasing those around us to other leaders who might serve them better is one of the things we have to evaluate.

We go through that transition with our children. As much as we love them, and as much as we want to guide them, there comes a time when they'll learn more by going off to college or into the workforce than they will by staying under our roof. And because we love them, we send them off. Sometimes with tears in our eyes, but we do send them.

Adding on: Moses and Jethro

Such a mind-set isn't limited to helping others find a better situation elsewhere under the guidance of someone else who can help them grow more fully. Usually, as we have discussed, mentor leaders will help people grow right where they are. Sometimes that involves enlisting more help in the effort.

In Moses' case, he had been leading on his own for years. He said, "The people come to me to get a ruling from God. When a dispute arises, they come to me, and I am the one who settles the case between the quarreling parties. I inform the people of God's decrees and give them his instructions" (Exodus 18:15-16).

His father-in-law, Jethro, however, had a better idea. He suggested that Moses select and mentor others to help him, that he build up other leaders—and their competence—so that they could share in the work God had set before him:

> *"This is not good!" Moses' father-in-law exclaimed. "You're going to wear yourself out—and the people, too. This job is too heavy a burden for you to handle all by yourself. Now listen to me, and let me give you a word of advice, and may God be with you. You should continue to be the people's representative before God, bringing their disputes to him. Teach them God's decrees, and give them his instructions. Show them how to conduct their lives. But select from all the people some capable, honest men who fear God and hate bribes. Appoint them as leaders over groups of one thousand, one hundred, fifty, and ten. They should always be available to solve the people's common disputes, but have them bring the major cases to you. Let the leaders decide the smaller matters themselves. They will help you carry the load, making the task easier for you. If you follow this advice, and if God commands you to do so, then you will be able to endure the pressures, and all these people will go home in peace."*
>
> EXODUS 18:17-23

Moses took the advice.

Mentor leaders should always look to add value to the lives of others, even if it means delegating authority to those they have mentored who are ready to be elevated to new levels of leadership responsibility.

Calling out: The Prodigal Brother

I spoke to the Minnesota Vikings at their chapel service before the first game of the 2009 season, and I told a familiar story, the story of the Prodigal Son from the Gospel of Luke, chapter 15. Most of the time when we hear this story, we highlight the younger son, who makes a mess of his life before returning home, or we focus on the father's response, which is a picture of God's response to us as our heavenly Father. He is filled with compassion, patience, and grace, even for a son who, frankly, doesn't deserve it. Like us.

But in my experience, the older brother in the story isn't talked about very much. He displays a "that's not fair" attitude when the father welcomes his younger brother back into the household, protesting his father's grace to the foolish one. But what about the leadership of the older brother? I suggested to the Vikings that he may have been *responsible* for his younger brother's wanderings. He at least could have tried to prevent him from wasting so much time on a dead-end journey. No one was in a better position than the older brother to mentor the younger brother. We don't know if he reinforced the father's goals and ideals or if he tried to counsel his younger brother before he left, but you wonder what might have happened if he had truly mentored him.

+ **We all have a role in leadership. We all can mentor.**

As I told the Vikings, we can't fall into the trap of only looking to the father as a possible mentor. It can't always be the teachers, the coaches, the supervisors, or the parents who are leading. Sometimes it has to be the older brother (or sister)—and all of us can fill that role at some time. We all have a role in leadership. We all can mentor. We all can create lives of value and create "coaching trees" of people whose lives we have affected.

By touching the lives of the people right around us, and by replicating leaders who in turn can replicate more leaders, we can create value far beyond the small sphere that we can reach and touch directly.

THE FINISH: LIVING A LIFE OF SIGNIFICANCE

The only ones among you who will be really happy are those who will have sought and found how to serve.

ALBERT SCHWEITZER

As I headed down the hall to the press conference to announce my retirement from the Indianapolis Colts, my assistant, Jackie Cook, pulled a letter from a stack of letters that had come in after the season concluded and told me I might want to take a moment to read it before I went into the press conference.

The letter was from a couple in Indiana. They weren't football fans. They rarely if ever watched Colts games, but they had been watching late-night cable television shortly after the Colts' loss to New England in "the Game of the Century" two years earlier and had seen a public service announcement—the one I had done for The Villages foster care home. The one I "didn't really have time to do" but did anyway.

Now, the letter informed me, they had a new twelve-year-old son in their home—a son who had never been coached in Little League, had never been on a vacation, had never had his own bed. Until now. They went on to tell me what a blessing this boy had become in their lives.

> ✢ We always have a platform. There is always someone whose life we can affect—even if we're not aware at the time that we're doing it.

That letter was a good reminder to me that we always have time. We always have a platform. There is always someone whose life we can affect—even if we're not aware at the time that we're doing it.

As I finished my remarks and stepped away from the podium one last time, I knew that our call to mentor others does not end with a "retirement" or any other life change we will go through. It's something we can do as long as we're breathing.

Usually we don't get a letter telling us of the eternal impact that one moment of our life has had. But that doesn't mean those moments don't happen, and it doesn't mean that a moment here, or fifteen minutes there, or even years of patient mentoring won't pay off down the road in ways we can't anticipate.

So we press on, with faith in things unseen, knowing that God walks with us and before us, guiding our steps as we use every opportunity to change lives around us.

Who knows which life will be different—for all eternity?

It very possibly could depend on us.

ACTION STEPS

1. Consider the ultimate outcome. The mentor leader's ultimate measure of success is simply this: Did you add value to the lives of others?

2. Focus on improvement. Regardless of "wins" and "losses," you have succeeded as a mentor leader if you have improved the lives of those you lead and of others who are affected by you and your "coaching tree."

3. Always be willing to find the right place for someone to serve, knowing that God has uniquely equipped every person with incredible gifts and abilities.

4. Prepare yourself to hand off your leadership to someone else who is ready to be elevated. Be ready to enlist the help of others, and then to call them out when needed.

5. There is always someone whose life you can affect for good. Do it!

6. It's not about us; it's about everything that God can do *through* us, *for* others.

7. At the end of it all, if even one life is better because we lived, our lives have significance.

Q & A WITH
TONY DUNGY

CHAPTER 1: THE MANDATE OF A MENTOR LEADER

1. *You mention your father, head coach Chuck Noll, and other mentor leaders who shaped your life. What characteristics did they have in common? What impact did they have on your spiritual life?*

Coach Noll and my dad were very much alike. They both were teachers and used teaching techniques in most situations. They didn't always just give advice or give me direct answers to my questions. They made me think and encouraged me to investigate and come up with my own answers. They both were very patient men. They talked about long-term plans and seeing the big picture. They were also very practical. By that, I mean they were able to help me in what was actually going on in my life at the moment. They both were willing to give their views on things, but always encouraged me to think for myself. I had other mentors who influenced me more spiritually, but the spiritual lessons I learned from my dad and Coach Noll were to put others first and to treat everyone as valuable in God's eyes. Tom Lamphere, our chaplain when I was with the Vikings, had a big impact on my spiritual life by reminding me that every decision I made had a spiritual component. He encouraged me to look at everything, including my coaching career, from a Christian perspective.

2. *How have you been able to balance time between coaching a successful pro football team and leading your own family and children? What difficulties did you have? How did you overcome them?*

Maintaining balance is the toughest thing to do. You realize that your family is the most important thing you have, but the job requires so much time. You want to do your best in both areas but find yourself spending much more time at work than at home. In the NFL, as with most jobs, you can't dictate the schedule. There were many weekends, evenings, and holidays when I had to be at work. I tried to become as efficient as I could and to be a good time manager at work. I didn't want to cheat my employer or my players, but I made it a priority not to waste time. I also made the decision to forgo some things away from work that I enjoyed, such as golf, to be home more. I tried to include my family in my job as much as possible. That wasn't too hard, because they all enjoy football. However, I really felt I had to do extra things when I was home to make my family understand that they were special, that they were a priority in my life.

3. *A lot of people view you as a truly exceptional coach and leader. But can the average person also become a mentor leader even*

if he or she doesn't share all of your skills or personality traits? What do you believe are the qualities a person needs?

I'm humbled anyone would think that about me. The biggest thing I try to do is to help other people. More than anything, that's what I saw in my parents. If you want to help people become the best they can be, they will gravitate to you. For me, that involved praying a lot, having God put that desire in my heart, and keeping it at the forefront of my mind. I also prayed for the ability to make good decisions and to lead in effective ways. I think God will help you that way as well. Being a good listener is also important. You can absorb helpful information and come up with good decisions by listening to other people.

4. *What would you say to the well-meaning father, mother, husband, or wife who believes that financial success will lead to a more secure and happy home?*

My first response would be something that Christ said: "What do you benefit if you gain the whole world but lose your own soul?" (Matthew 16:26). Many of us think that having a great career, making enough money so we can take care of our family's physical needs, and having enough money in the bank to feel "secure" will lead us to happiness. I've found that's not always the case. First of all, those things—career, homes, wealth—can be taken from us in a moment. And they also will not be emotionally or spiritually satisfying. I've seen too many people who had all the material things they could want and were very unhappy with their lives because they found they weren't fulfilled. One of the best pieces of advice Coach Noll ever gave me was not to make any career decisions based on money. Don't look at salary or security as the most important thing. Rather, before accepting a job, look at what you will learn from that employer, the type of people you will be around, and how it will help you reach your long-term life goals. And he was right. You can't totally disregard salary, but it can't be the most important thing in your decision-making process. You have to trust that God will take care of your family's needs.

5. *How can one learn to shift from a position-centered leadership style to relationship-driven mentor leadership?*

   Just think about the people who have had the most positive impact in your life. Think of what you have learned from them and how they got those messages across to you. When I started coaching, I thought about the coaches who had helped me the most and whom I really enjoyed playing for. I decided to use that as my coaching style. I also thought about lessons and techniques I'd learned from other coaches whom I may not have enjoyed as much but who had given me valuable information. Could I get that information to my players but do it in a way that would be more helpful? I also made a conscious decision to go against the grain of conventional wisdom and continue to foster relationships with the players and coaches I was working with. To me, that was very normal, but it went against a lot of the advice I got from people early in my career, who said you had to keep a certain amount of space between yourself and your players. "You don't want them to be too comfortable around you." But I felt the better I knew my players, the more I could help them become a better team.

6. *You mention your involvement in prison ministry. What are some practical ways in which ordinary men and women can begin to develop mentoring relationships through similar ministries and organizations?*

   A lot of organizations that focus on helping people rely on volunteers. Whether it's a prison outreach, a youth or senior citizen outreach, or a church group, I think that by working in these types of environments you can really help others as you grow yourself. Some of the most rewarding experiences I've had were talking to people in these settings. It makes you think about your priorities in life and causes you to evaluate the advice you're giving. By volunteering, you can also control the amount of time you give. But be careful, because you may find you enjoy it so much you'll be tempted to give up your full-time job, just as I did.

7. *Why is it so important to "get our hands dirty" living life alongside those we mentor?*

Young people, especially today, are not impressed by "tell me what to do." They are much more engaged with "show me what to do and how to do it." Those you mentor want to feel that you really know what they're going through and that you can understand the questions they're asking. The way to do that is to be there, to be involved, and to show them you care by spending time with them. The other benefit of being right there with those we mentor is that we will actually learn some new things ourselves. By observing and listening to them, many times I find out things I would never have known otherwise.

8. *Did you ever struggle to maintain a long-term perspective while mentoring your players and others you knew? How did you overcome that?*

I always tried to think long-term because so many of the people in my life encouraged me to do that. But it's not always easy—especially with young people, because they're looking for answers right now. I try to remember that when I was younger, I was that way myself!

CHAPTER 2: THE MIND-SET OF A MENTOR LEADER

1. *In the high-pressure world of the NFL, how did you keep your focus on establishing a lasting legacy rather than succumbing to organizational pressures to win?*

   Coaches are judged on winning, and that's important, but I felt we would win more consistently if we stayed true to the goal of building a great organization. I didn't want to fall into the trap of making short-term adjustments for the benefit of one season. It's hard to keep that focus, especially if you have some disappointing seasons. But fortunately, I worked with people who had the same idea in mind, to be as consistently good as possible. Then my job was merely to keep everyone focused on that goal and not to look at quick-fix ideas or succumb to the pressure to change. We knew we had a good plan that would stand the test of time if we persevered.

2. *You mention some of the different leadership styles used by mentor leaders. Does your leadership change depending on whether you're working with your players, your colleagues, your children, or someone in a more formal mentoring relationship, such as Michael Vick?*

   I don't think my tone changes, but you do have to keep in mind the needs and the maturity of the group you're leading. I'm always following the path of my parents and trying to help my groups learn as they go, to develop confidence in themselves, and to become good decision makers. Sometimes that involves more encouragement, sometimes more discipline or direction, and sometimes more role modeling. But the underlying tone is the same, and my motivation is the same—to help them become the best they can be.

3. *Have you ever had a time when you almost walked away "just before the break of dawn"? What was the outcome of the situation?*

There are many times when you don't feel as if you can get over the hump, whether it's perfecting a skill on the athletic field, learning a concept in school, or getting through to a talented individual who is not performing up to potential. I've learned over the years to pray for perseverance in those situations. Probably the biggest example that comes to mind is when I decided to quit my high school football team before my senior year because I wasn't sure about my relationship with my coach. Fortunately, I had some people around me who talked me into not giving up so quickly, and it certainly changed the course of my adult life.

4. *What makes for an effective mission statement?*

Mission statements are very simple. They explain what you are or your organization is all about at the very core. An effective mission statement will let you know what is really important about what you're doing. It will allow you to stay focused when you have to make decisions about which direction to go. Ask, "Will this path help me or hurt me on my journey to fulfilling my mission?"

5. *In John 13, Jesus kneels before His disciples and washes their feet. What do you hope people can take away from Jesus' powerful example?*

Christ said He, as the ultimate leader, had set an example by serving. It was a reminder that the most effective leaders, who will have the most effective teams, will base their approach not on ego or position but on commitment to other people and making other people better.

6. *Are there any practical benefits of being in a position of service rather than a position of authority?*

Authority and leadership sometimes come with position. When you're the head coach, you have authority over the team. But even though the players must submit to your authority, it doesn't mean they will respect your leadership. The best way to create an environment where people willingly follow your leadership is to let them know that your number one priority is to help them. And there's no better way to show that than by demonstrating your desire to serve.

CHAPTER 3: THE MATURITY OF A MENTOR LEADER

1. *If people are unwilling to think through their pasts and forgive themselves and others, how will this hinder their ability to be strong mentor leaders?*

Confidence is a trait that people look for in their leaders. You have to feel good about yourself and where you're going to lead effectively. If you don't get over past failures, learn from them, and move on with confidence, it will be hard to lead. Everyone makes mistakes. My goal in letting people know that I've made mistakes is to help them avoid making the same ones. My shortfalls can help others. I think that's one of the reasons God allows disappointments in our lives.

2. *How were you able to strike a healthy balance between your passions and your priorities in your career?*

I think God gives us passions, and that is great. That's what makes us tick. We just have to keep those passions in the right spot in our lives. There's a fine line between passion and addiction, between a dedicated employee and a workaholic. I pray constantly for balance in my life, thanking God for the things

I enjoy but asking Him to help me keep them in perspective. It also helps to have someone—your spouse or a close friend— who is able to tell you honestly how you're doing.

3. *What lessons can we learn from mentor leaders who know they don't have all the answers, but who still are constantly looking for ways to grow?*

When I was younger, I used to shake my head at my dad. I couldn't wait to stop going to school, and yet he was always taking more courses, even after he had received his PhD. But he didn't want to shortchange his students. What if there was something new in the biology field that he wasn't up on? Not only would he miss it, but his students would be disadvantaged. It took me a while to understand that, but when I started coaching it began to make sense. I couldn't undermine my players' ability to perform at their best because I hadn't taken the time to keep learning more about football. The more you know, the better you'll be able to teach.

4. *Why do you think so many leaders have a difficult time admitting their weaknesses? Are there constructive, loving ways that their colleagues and friends can help?*

Number one, it's human nature not to talk about our weaknesses. We want people to know our strengths. As leaders, we've also been taught not to give any appearance of vulnerability— we always have to appear as if we have the answer to everything. That's not possible, of course, but that's the image we feel we have to portray. Many times, as leaders, it's tough to get honest, constructive criticism from the people around us. They're afraid of how we might respond. When I was an assistant coach, I used to have great talks with my fellow staff members about how we would improve the way we did things if we were in charge. Of course, we would never go to the head coach and tell him that, even though we knew that some of our ideas could help the team. Then, when I became the head coach, the same guys were hesitant to come to me because now *I* was the boss. But it's important to create a climate in which people feel they can come to you with constructive criticism. It's the only way we can all improve.

5. *In order to form a cohesive team of individuals with complementary strengths, is it also necessary to detach ourselves from damaging or negative relationships?*

I talked to my teams about relationships all the time. Our goal has to be for the team to function well. Anything that detracts from that hurts our mission. That includes our relationships. It's hard to tell people (especially adults) who their friends should be or whom they should associate with. But those relationships will affect their performance and eventually affect the performance of the team. Part of being a mentor leader is getting that message across.

CHAPTER 4: THE MARKS OF A MENTOR LEADER

1. *One of the relational qualities you describe is character. How is character different from integrity? What are some ways a mentor can encourage others to develop their character?*

Integrity is part of character. In fact, it's the biggest part. If you have integrity, that's going to impact everything you do and make you a person of high character. But character is all-encompassing. Are you going to be a good teammate? Are you going to help others be better? Are you hardworking, someone who will persevere through tough times? Are you a person who's going to put the team first, ahead of your individual goals?

These are facets of character that are separate from integrity. You may be one of the most honest people in the world, but that alone won't make you a good teammate.

2. *Many people are evaluated on the basis of their professional "win/loss record." Should character also be a factor when reviewing performance? How can that be accomplished?*

   There's no question that character has to be considered. How you accomplish your goals is more important in the long run than merely getting to the top by any means possible. We're seeing that today in the debate about certain baseball stars being selected to the Hall of Fame after they've been found to have used performance-enhancing drugs. Ben Roethlisberger has quarterbacked the Pittsburgh Steelers to two Super Bowl wins, but the people of Pittsburgh have been turned off by some of his off-field problems. More and more often people are coming to the conclusion that character has to be part of our evaluation of performance.

3. *Accountability is often a difficult leadership trait to practice. Why do you think this is so, and what can be done to make it easier?*

   We are generally held accountable at work by our superiors. We have to report to them, and they are responsible for evaluating our performance. As we attain leadership positions, there are fewer and fewer people to hold us accountable. In our personal lives, very few people have access to our lives to really know how we are living. We have to initiate that type of relationship by intentionally allowing certain people access into our thoughts and deeds. It isn't easy because we don't want to tell people our faults and shortcomings. We have to find someone we trust and someone who cares enough about us to ask the tough questions. Someone who knows us well enough to tell when we're being open and honest. Someone who will stick with you. It's not easy to find such a person, but it's important. If you're married, don't neglect the role of your spouse in this process. He or she knows you better and cares about you more than anyone else. My wife definitely helps me stay on track and helps me stay on the lookout for problem areas in my life.

4. *If leaders feel they have made mistakes that have damaged their integrity, what can they do to correct the situation? How might they use their experience in mentoring others?*

    As the Bible points out, the first thing we have to do is admit the mistake to ourselves and to God. Then we have to acknowledge it to the people we've affected. That's the toughest part. Many times, it's embarrassing or may be hurtful to people we're close to—family, friends, or coworkers. However, once we get through the initial pain, those relationships will grow stronger. If we're honest and sincere, we may be surprised by how willing people are to forgive. Those situations can be used greatly when we're mentoring others. We can acknowledge that no one is perfect and that maintaining our integrity is critical. We can encourage them by admitting some of our own mistakes and showing how we were able to overcome them.

5. *How has understanding the importance of being available and approachable strengthened your mentoring relationships?*

    Whether it's with my children, friends, staff, or coworkers, being available and approachable are the two most important components of helping someone. If people feel you're approachable, they will be at ease and feel good about sharing with you and learning from you. At the same time, you may be the most approachable person in the world, but if you're not available, it doesn't help. So you have to pick your spots, because there are so many opportunities to mentor. For me, I have to constantly take inventory of my time, because I want to make sure I'm available for my children and not neglect their need to have me as the leader of the household.

6. *Do you agree with Jim Zorn's practice to "act medium"?*

"Acting medium" is a great principle, but it's tough to do. I've always tried to keep on an even keel myself, and I encouraged my teams to do the same. When we had big wins, I wanted us to enjoy them—God calls us to a joyful life, after all—but not get so excited that we didn't continue to prepare ourselves for the following week's game. If we lost, I never wanted the players to act as if it were the end of the world. We could learn from our losses and improve the next week. It's the same thing in life, but it goes against our human nature. We're emotional creatures, and we are going to have highs and lows. We just have to try not to let those highs and lows affect us too much.

7. *Are there certain things a mentor can do to demonstrate loyalty? Is it of equal importance that those being mentored also show loyalty?*

Loyalty means being there for other people, supporting them and sticking with them no matter what. The way you demonstrate loyalty is by your actions. You have to let people know that you're there *for them*—not because it benefits you. Being consistently available is important, as is being available in the tough times as well as the good times. Confidentiality is also critical—keep things that are supposed to be private from getting out to others. Of course, loyalty is a two-way street, but as the mentor you may have to take the lead in demonstrating how to show loyalty.

8. *Do you believe a mentoring relationship can exist without any one of the leadership traits, attributes, and qualities you describe in chapter 4? Why or why not?*

Yes, I think you can mentor and help people without all of those attributes, but the relationship will be maximized when all the qualities are there. That's when the person being mentored will get the most out of it.

CHAPTER 5: THE MOMENTS OF A MENTOR LEADER

1. *What is a platform? What do you think is your platform as a mentor leader? Can one's platform change over time?*

A platform is merely the place where God puts you and the space you have to exercise your gifts and influence people. We all have one. We have a circle in which we travel where we impact others. It could be at home with family, at school with our fellow students, or at work with coworkers or customers. We don't really know the full scope of our platform because as we influence one person we have an indirect influence on other people. My high school football coach, for example, couldn't have known when he gave some advice to me during my sophomore year that I would repeat that advice to hundreds of NFL players over the next thirty years.

2. *What would you say to a mature young man or woman who would like to be a mentor to his or her younger friends?*

I would say to step out and not be afraid to do that. I have shared how my life was affected by people who reached out to me when I was growing up. Due to the number of broken homes in our society, we need mentoring more than ever today, because so many of our young people aren't getting that guidance from their parents.

3. *Amid the busyness of your personal and family life, do you ever find it difficult to focus on having an impact on others? How do you handle it?*

Yes, it's easy to get busy and to get caught up in your own schedule and personal needs. I try to read the Bible every day, and that helps me to stay on course and look for opportunities to help others. The Bible always reminds me of why God put us here—to be leaders of our families, to help others, and to point people to Christ.

4. *What are some consequences of not recognizing an opportunity for influence?*

When we help someone, we may get positive feedback—a letter or an e-mail thanking us. But we don't always see the ramifications of *not* helping someone in need—or worse, of being a negative influence. I can only think of some of the poor decisions I might have made, had someone not been there to lead me. I know how much I owe to those people, and that's what motivates me to look for similar opportunities to influence others.

5. *Are you ever wary of labeling public figures and famous celebrities as role models for young people? What do you think are the dangers of seeing them as role models? What are the benefits?*

No matter how we look at it, those people *are* role models. They have a tremendous influence on our young people. This can be a great benefit because they can reach our youth and get a message across to them. The danger is that it may be the wrong message. We have to try to get our young people to examine their heroes and follow those people who have the right lifestyle and the right message.

6. *How can Christians demonstrate their character to colleagues, teammates, and opponents who do not share the same values?*

People want to see if our actions match our words. I've always felt that the most important thing I could do was to live out my Christian beliefs amid the people I'm in contact with. Then, if they see something attractive in my life and ask where it comes from, I can share that it's because of my relationship with Jesus Christ. But I find that my actions and my attitude speak louder than my words.

7. *We've all seen or heard of coaches—even Christian ones—who permit, tolerate, or encourage dirty or aggressive play in order to achieve the goal of winning. Is there any validity to their apparent belief that "it's all part of the game"?*

One of the things I think is very important in sports (and also in life) is to win with class and integrity. If you don't do it the right way, if you teach your players that anything goes as long as you win, you're leading them down a dangerous path. There's a difference between aggressive play and dirty play. If you break the rules, it will eventually come back to haunt you, in sports or in life.

8. *How can coaches teach their teams to display Christian character but still play tough?*

There is nothing in the Bible about Christian character that says we shouldn't play tough. One of my favorite passages is 1 Corinthians 9:24-27, in which Paul says that we are to "run to win!" But as we're doing our best at everything we do, we have to keep in mind not only the rules of the game but also God's rules. We can be tough, and we can be winners, and still show others what it means to be a Christian.

CHAPTER 6: THE MODEL OF A MENTOR LEADER

1. *Do you believe that mentors need their own mentors in order to stay accountable and to make sure their actions match their words?*

   Yes, it's important for all of us to have other people who are helping us grow, looking out for us, and keeping us focused. We should never think we've come to a place in life where we don't need that.

2. *You mention that faith is the foundation and strength of a mentor leader. How has faith helped you coach your teams through difficult seasons? How have you relied on faith to lead your family?*

   An athletic season is never a completely smooth road, and neither is life. There will be ups and downs, disappointments and challenges, and our perseverance is going to be tested. My Christian faith is what has helped me get through those tough times, on the field and off. I believe that God wants me to keep going, to set a good example, and to rely on Him in the tough times. That's what I've tried to do in leading my teams, and it's the same attitude my wife and I have tried to instill in our children.

3. *How should mentor leaders react when someone under their leadership blatantly disregards their authority or is disrespectful? Can you give an example of how you handled such a situation?*

   As the leader, you have to confront situations where people aren't following your design or are being disrespectful to you or others in the group. But the goal has to be to make the situation better. I've always tried to find out why the person is behaving in that manner and to explain what the team needs in order to be successful. In 2003, when I was coaching the Colts, we had an incident in which one of our players made some statements to the media questioning my leadership as well as that of our quarterback, Peyton Manning. Most people told me I should get rid of that player immediately, but I wanted to see what was in his heart and what was behind the statements he had made. We talked it out, and I came to the conclusion there was some frustration and some bad judgment involved. We were able to straighten out some hurt feelings, and he went on to have his best year the next season.

4. *How would you counsel an athlete who wonders, "Does my behavior on the field reflect Christian values?" What does that mean when you're in the heat of the battle?*

As a Christian, I think I have to display the characteristics that please God all the time. That includes in the heat of battle. It's not easy, and times of high emotion can cause us to do things we later regret. But just like anything else, the more we practice the better we get. So, we have to *practice* staying under control in high-pressure situations. Many people comment on my calm demeanor during games, but I wasn't always like that. It's something I worked on and improved because I felt it was an important part of my Christian witness.

5. *For coaches who are trying to be mentor leaders, how should they "manage" referees and umpires? Where is the line between arguing a call and defending a player?*

There is nothing wrong with disagreeing with an umpire or a referee, or standing up for your players. It's all in how you do it. I believe I got my points across to officials, and did my job for our players, without using profanity or trying to embarrass an official. Again, I think it's important when you're the leader to lead in the right way in all situations.

CHAPTER 7: THE MEANS OF A MENTOR LEADER

1. *What did Jim Irsay mean when he said he wanted to "change the culture" and build an organization that stood for something beyond football?*

   He knew that the Colts did not have a long history with their fans in Indianapolis. He wanted to develop a winning team, but more than that, he wanted to connect with the fans. He wanted the city to embrace the players for who they were and how they carried themselves in the community, not just for how much they won.

2. *What problems do you see permeating the culture in America's workplaces and in our families?*

   Many of the problems we're seeing in the workplace go back to the problems we're experiencing with our family units. Many of our children are not being mentored properly early in life. Whether it's because of the time parents have to spend working, or because of the breakdown of the American family, our kids are not being taught the core values that will help them succeed in the workplace. Honesty, hard work, teamwork, and reliability are values we should learn very early in life. They are the foundation for productivity. I think we have to do a better job of getting that message across to young people who may not have gotten it from their parents.

3. *Have you ever faced resistance when trying to build a team that represents a variety of backgrounds, strengths, and weaknesses? How have you dealt with this?*

   Sure. Not everyone buys into the idea that diversity is important to success. I tried to show how the complementary strengths of people with different experiences and backgrounds would help us in the long run and to be consistent in emphasizing the common values that defined us as a team. I also looked for people who were willing to work together and blend their individual talents with others for the good of the team.

4. *Do you think coaches in particular have a hard time hearing correction and constructive criticism?*

Coaches are no different from anyone else. We think we have the right ideas and that our way is the best way. It takes a certain amount of self-confidence to be a successful coach, but it also takes humility to realize the ways in which you can improve. The best coaches are the ones who keep their core values in place but continue to adapt and improve—and that means listening to constructive criticism.

CHAPTER 8: THE METHODS OF A MENTOR LEADER

1. *Are there certain boundaries that exist in mentor leadership? How does one navigate these? What advice would you give to mentor leaders who are unsure of how much to engage in other people's lives?*

Yes, it is important to have appropriate boundaries in a mentoring relationship. But the important thing in building relationships is to do everything you can for the *benefit* of the other person. If you keep that in mind, you'll never cross the line and go beyond where you should.

2. *What are some practical ways in which mentor leaders can create an environment that equips their teams to thrive and be successful?*

Lead by example. Make sure that you're doing the things you're telling your group to do. Make sure you keep articulating the mission statement. This can be done in a number of ways, including signs in the office or on notebooks—anything to keep the message of what you're trying to accomplish in front of your group. Do things to stimulate dialogue. They can be planned events or in informal settings (as Mr. Rockquemore did with my friends and me in junior high), but let your people know that you want to hear their thoughts—both positive and negative—expressed in a way that will help the group.

3. *How can mentor leaders strike the right balance between encouragement and constructive criticism?*

I always have to remind myself to praise people and let them know when they're doing a good job. We expect things to go well, and when they do we don't comment. That can lead to a habit of only correcting people or only commenting when things aren't done right. Without realizing it, we can come across as being totally negative when that's not our intent at all. There will be times when you have to correct people, so make sure you balance those times with times of encouragement and praise.

CHAPTER 9: THE MEASURE OF A MENTOR LEADER

1. *How can mentor leaders know that they have added value to the lives of others?*

You don't always know. You just have to do what you feel in your heart is right and trust God that you are helping others. You can see performance, and that is somewhat of an indicator. But the true life lessons, the things that are really meaningful in the long run, sometimes will take a while to come out in the people you're mentoring. However, there's nothing like a phone call or a letter that comes years down the road from someone who says that you helped in some small way. When you get some positive feedback, it makes all your efforts seem worth it.

2. *While you have been able to encourage, empower, and educate countless people over the years, what are some lessons that these same people have taught you?*

   I've learned that people can usually do more than they think they can, and many times more than I think they can. Sometimes, they just need the right spark. I've also learned that people who are motivated to do well will generally find a way to succeed. But perhaps the biggest thing I've learned is that it is such a great feeling to see the people you work with experience success, especially when those relationships go deeper than simply that of an employer and employee.

3. *What would you say to people who are having doubts about whether they can truly make a positive difference in the lives of others? Did you ever face similar doubts?*

   There will always be times when we feel less than adequate trying to help other people. If someone asked me to help a young man become a better football player, I have no doubt that I could do that. I believe that's my area of expertise. But take that to other areas, and I become much less confident. What I have to remember is that I may not have all the answers, but that's okay. If I don't know, I can at least point the person in the right direction. And most times, I end up helping more than I thought I could.

4. *In this chapter, you share the story of Jethro and Moses and the example of John the Baptist, leaders who gladly deferred their own status of power to others. Have you ever had to do*

*the same in your coaching career or in your role as a mentor
to young men?*

Yes. I always wanted assistant coaches to come to our staff
and grow. If they excelled, I thought it helped us as a team.
It allowed me to delegate responsibility and be more efficient
as a leader. I never worried that our owner or our players
would think any less of me because we had strong assistants. I have enjoyed training other coaches and seeing them
go off and embark on successful careers, even though their
success could come back to haunt my teams. One of my most
painful days in football was during the 2002 playoffs when
the New York Jets, coached by Herman Edwards, one of my
former assistants, beat our team 41–0. But as disappointed as
I was, I was happy for Herm—he had learned his lessons . . .
too well!

5. *What has been the most fulfilling part of being a mentor leader
for you?*

For me, the real joy is seeing a person come to our team and
leave as a better player and a more mature person. Seeing those
individuals grow is great. Then, seeing how those individuals
come together and function as a unit—with a single purpose
in mind—and have some success and develop lifelong friendships; for me, it doesn't get any better than that. Outside of the
team setting, seeing someone feeling better about themselves,
becoming more whom God intended them to be—whatever
their age—makes it all worthwhile.

ABOUT THE AUTHORS

TONY DUNGY is the #1 *New York Times* best-selling author of *Quiet Strength* and *Uncommon*. He led the Indianapolis Colts to Super Bowl victory on February 4, 2007, the first such win for an African American head coach. Dungy established another NFL first by becoming the first head coach to lead his teams to the playoffs for ten consecutive years.

Dungy joined the Colts in 2002 after serving as the most successful head coach in Tampa Bay Buccaneers history. He has also held assistant coaching positions with the University of Minnesota, Pittsburgh Steelers, Kansas City Chiefs, and Minnesota Vikings. Before becoming a coach, Dungy played three seasons in the NFL.

Dungy has been involved in a wide variety of charitable organizations, including All Pro Dad, Abe Brown Ministries, Fellowship of Christian Athletes, Athletes in Action, Mentors for Life, Big Brothers Big Sisters, and Boys & Girls Clubs. He also works with Basket of Hope, Impact for Living, the Black Coaches Association National Convention, Indiana Black Expo, the United Way of Central Indiana, and the American Diabetes Association.

He retired from coaching in 2009 and now serves as a studio analyst for NBC's *Football Night in America*. He and his wife, Lauren, are the parents of seven children.

NATHAN WHITAKER is the coauthor of *Quiet Strength* and *Uncommon* and a Harvard Law School graduate whose firm currently represents NFL and college coaches and administrators. A two-sport athlete in baseball and football at Duke University, he has worked in football administration for the Jacksonville Jaguars and Tampa Bay Buccaneers. He lives in Florida with his wife, Amy, and their two daughters, Hannah and Ellie Kate. Visit him online at www.nathanwhitaker.com, www.impactforliving.org, and www.sixseeds.tv.

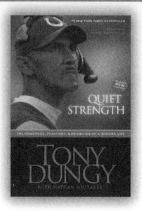
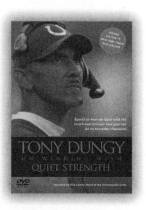
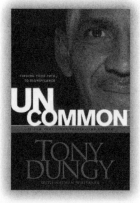

An entirely new football experience!

Tony Dungy's RED ZONE is a theater-and-DVD event born out of a tremendous love for the game of football and a strong desire to support parents and coaches in their quest for positive role models. Get inside tips from the pros on conditioning, increasing performance and mental toughness, and viewing football as training for life. Designed especially for student-athletes, this resource will inspire and motivate youth-through-high-school football players and teams.

Go to www.redzonelive.com to learn more!

Tony Dungy, NFL head coach and Super Bowl XLI champion, brings together his faith, love of children, and love of sports to tell a story of inspiration and encouragement.

Available everywhere books are sold.

Look for *You Can Be a Friend!*—the new children's book from Lauren and Tony Dungy—coming in January 2011!